C000071192

PUBLISHED FOR THE MALONE SOCIETY BY
OXFORD UNIVERSITY PRESS

WALTON STREET, OXFORD OX2 6DP

Oxford New York Toronto
Delhi Bombay Calcutta Karachi
Petaling Jaya Singapore Hong Kong Tokyo
Nairobi Dar es Salaam Cape Town
Melbourne Auckland

and associated companies in
Berlin Ibadan

ISBN 0 19 729030 2

Printed by BAS Printers Limited, Over Wallop, Hampshire

TOM A LINCOLN

THE MALONE SOCIETY
REPRINTS
1992

This edition of *Tom a Lincoln*, a hitherto unpublished and untitled Jacobean play, was prepared by G. R. Proudfoot. H. R. Woudhuysen and the General Editor assisted with its preparation, and checked the edition.

The Society is grateful to the British Library for permission to edit the text and reproduce pages from its manuscript, Add. 61745.

August 1991 JOHN PITCHER

CONTENTS

PREFACE

THE manuscript which contains the unique copy of the Jacobean play here printed for the first time, under the editorial title of *Tom a Lincoln*, was discovered in 1973 among the papers of Sir John Coke, Secretary of State in the reign of Charles I. In 1980 it was acquired by the British Library, and was made available for study in 1982, with the number Add. 61745.

As well as the text of the play, there are eleven items in the manuscript. These include verses in English and Welsh, an inventory of books, jottings, payments, and memoranda. A fuller understanding of the origins of the play—its authorship, transcription, and context—may be derived from these items. For this reason the present edition contains edited texts of the complete contents of the manuscript. Further work in English and Welsh archives, especially legal ones, may help to elucidate the connections between the writer(s) and the scribes of this play.

In the course of preparing this edition Professor Proudfoot has received assistance from several individuals. He wishes to thank in particular Ceridwen Lloyd-Morgan of the National Library of Wales for revising the text and literal translation of the Welsh verses, and for her guidance and comments on these poems and the manuscript's Welsh connections; Patrick Ford of the University of California, Los Angeles, who supplied the first texts and translations of the Welsh material; and Arthur Kinney and the Renaissance Text Society of America for inviting him to lecture on the play at the Newberry Library on 23 January 1986. Thanks are also due to: Janet Bately, Roy Booth, Muriel Bradbrook, David Carnegie, Sandra Clark, Janet Cowen, Alan Dessen, Arthur Freeman, Gareth Roberts, Jane Roberts, Gary Taylor, Joanna Udall, Stanley Wells, and Marion Wynne-Davies.

INTRODUCTION

The Manuscript

Provenance

THE manuscript was discovered in 1973 among the papers of Sir John Coke (1563–1644), Secretary of State in the reign of Charles I, at his country home, Melbourne Hall in Derbyshire. The papers in question were apparently transferred to Melbourne Hall in 1634 from Gray's Inn, where Coke's son Thomas was in residence. The manuscript was offered for sale at Sotheby's in London on 20 November 1973. An extended and informative catalogue description by the late P. J. Croft, subsequently Librarian of King's College, Cambridge, identified the play as one of the many unknown works of the dramatist Thomas Heywood, who was, on his own evidence, sole or part author of over two hundred plays.[1]

The manuscript was sold on 20 November to the New York dealer, John Fleming, who was acting on behalf of the Folger Shakespeare Library. At a meeting on 11 January 1974 the British Export Licensing Review Committee held up the licence for two months in case any British institution could equal the offer made by Fleming.[2] The sale fell through when an anonymous private English purchaser came forward with an offer to match the price and give the manuscript to the Bodleian Library. By the time that this offer had fallen through, the American purchasers had also lost interest and the manuscript remained with Sotheby's throughout the 1970s. It is said to have been withdrawn from sale by its owner, the Marquess of Lothian. The interest which the manuscript had aroused at the end of 1973 died down with its disappearance

[1] The fact that the notebook of Morgan Evans was found among the papers of Sir John Coke remains puzzling. What evidence there is suggests that the play was copied into the manuscript before the dated entries on Fols. 50a, 51a and 61b, that is, before 1616–19. The manuscript must therefore have remained in Evans' possession at least until 1619. Coke himself is not known to have been in London for some years after his marriage in 1605 (he refused the invitation of Fulke Greville to visit him there in 1610: see R. A. Rebholz, *The Life of Fulke Greville* (Oxford, 1971), p. 197). It is worth noting that another dramatic manuscript, the alleged Webster fragment, also came from this same Lothian source: see, Antony Hammond and Doreen DelVecchio, 'The Melbourne Manuscript and John Webster: A Reproduction and Transcript', *Studies in Bibliography* 41 (1988), 1–32.

[2] Information from M. C. Bradbrook, 'A New Jacobean Play from the Inns of Court', *Shakespearean Research and Opportunities*, 7–8 (1972–74), 1–5. The play was read in 1973 by Mr Croft and Dr Daniel Waley, Keeper of Manuscripts at the British Library. The conjecture published in Professor Bradbrook's article was based, as she took pains to point out, on Croft's description in the sale catalogue, and on conversations with Dr Waley.

from public view. Its acquisition by the British Library on 14 March 1980 passed unnoted.

An important clue to the origin of the manuscript is the name 'Morganus: Evans:', which is written at the end of the play's epilogue (Fol. 46b, line 3095). Croft identified Morgan Evans as the son and heir of John Evans of Lantwit Major, county Glamorgan, gentleman, who entered Gray's Inn as a student on 7 June 1607. There is, however, at least one other Morgan Evans whose dates and circumstances agree with those of the manuscript. This is the son and heir of John Evans of Llancoyd-vauder, county Glamorgan, who matriculated, aged 15, at Hart Hall in Oxford on 24 November 1599. He received his BA from St Edmund Hall on 11 February 1601–2, and may have been a student of Gray's Inn in 1605.[3]

Memoranda on Fols. 48–9 and 61b of the manuscript are couched as the notes of a son about to visit London who has been tasked with seeking legal advice, on his father's behalf, about a number of matters concerning the family estate. Unfortunately, none of these memoranda include place names with which either of these Morgan Evanses, or others, might be easily identified. The personal names in the notes, however, indicate a provenance in North East Wales: the one named town, Bishops Castle, is in Shropshire near the Welsh border.[4] The handwriting of the memoranda may well be a scribbled version of Hand A, the scribe who copied over half of the play and who is clearly Evans himself. It is reasonable to assume that the miscellaneous short entries in the latter part of the manuscript were made after most of it had been used for the text of the play. The two Welsh poems transcribed on Fols. 62b–63a are not listed in the first-line index of Welsh poetry in manuscript (although the index is currently being corrected and revised at the National Library of Wales).

The connection of the play with Gray's Inn seems well established. The manuscript was found among papers which had their origin there, and the play is subscribed by Morgan Evans, who was its principal copyist, and who may have been a student of the Inn. It bears the traces of an entertainment which would have been appropriate to a Christmas Revel at the Inn. Most obvious

[3] For Evans of Lantwit Major (Llanilltyd Fawr), see J. Foster, *The Register of Admissions to Gray's Inn, 1521–1889* (London, 1889), p. 110; for Evans of Llancoyd-vauder (Llanilltyd Faedre), see *Alumni Oxonienses*, 4 vols., ed. J. Foster (London, 1891), ii. 471.

[4] Apart from 'bushop Castle' (item beginning on Fol. 48a, ll. 19–20), and perhaps 'Ryswyn' (56), the place names seem to be those of farms: 'can dw poub' (3), 'Cwmgwernog' (18), 'Ty Kan y lan' (66), and 'Calbioch' (94). The personal names carry a range of local suggestions. Ednevet (Ednyfed) is commonest in north-eastern and eastern Wales; Lloyds are usually from Denbighshire or Montgomeryshire; Jarman is strongly associated with Montgomeryshire; the Christian name Winifred is very rare at this period in Wales as a whole and may suggest at least a connection with Flintshire, site of St Winifred's Well at Holywell. (Information from Dr C. Lloyd-Morgan, private communication, 28 April 1991.)

of these is the epilogue, in which the actor who played the clown, Rusticano, offers the play and its performers for judgement by the 'Courteous hearers'. His speech is full of legal vocabulary and allusion (see lines 3064–75, 3081–7). Equally distinctive are the lines in Rusticano's drinking song, 'yor drunkard is a lawyer/there is none thats heere but knowe him' (lines 1516–17).

Legal jokes are sprinkled throughout the text: 'termers' are mistaken for 'turners', for example (Fol. 8b: line 478), and Latin legal tags are frequently quoted or distorted. Muriel Bradbrook has argued that the play may even have been intended as a covert satire on Lincoln's Inn.[5] It is tempting to go further, and conjecture that the names and treatment of two subsidiary characters in the play contain allusions to, and even satire of, contemporary figures within Gray's Inn itself. On the final written page of the manuscript, Evans lists 'my bookes & such things I left behinde mee in my study at my goinge home, wich I Committed to the Custidy of Sir Walwine' (Fol. 63b, lines 1–3). Croft suggested that 'Sir Walwine' might refer to Thomas Walwyn, who matriculated at Clare College, Cambridge, in Michaelmas 1579, and who was admitted to Gray's Inn on 28 October 1584.[6] It is certainly true that the author of the play replaced one character he found in his source, Sir Triamore, with Sir Gawain or, as his name is spelt in the play, 'Sir Gallowine'. There is no obvious reason why he should have done this, unless it was indeed to allude to Thomas Walwyn, who was a senior member of the Inn. Similarly, the jokes against Sir Lancelot —too unattractive as a marriage prospect for Angelica in the opening scene, and later mocked by the clown as 'lance-lout' (lines 94–106, and 1916–20)— might well be instances of student humour, conceivably directed at Lancelot Lovelace, reader at Gray's Inn in 1609.[7]

Paper, Contents, and Make-up

British Library manuscript Add. 61745 is a small quarto book of sixty-four leaves, originally bound in a soft vellum cover. The wrapper and the gatherings of the manuscript have each been separately mounted and restored in a modern binding since the acquisition of the manuscript by the British Library.

A single stock of paper is used throughout. The watermark is a horn surmounted by a fool's cap within a heraldic shield, with a C (or G) to the left and a D to the right of the fool's cap. The mark shares the basic design of Churchill 313, found by him in a document dated 1620 in Worcester Cathedral Library, and identified as coming from the mill of Giles Duran.[8]

[5] 'A New Jacobean Play', p. 4.

[6] Croft, p. 6. Foster, *Register*, p. 66, describes Thomas Walwyn as 'of Arundel, Sussex, late of Staple Inn, gent.'.

[7] Foster, *Register*, p. 59, records Lovelace's entry, 7 June 1581, as of 'Chawlke, Kent, late of Staple Inn'.

[8] W. A. Churchill, *Watermarks in Paper in Holland, England, France, etc* (Amsterdam, 1935).

The contents of the manuscript comprise:

Folio	*Contents*
1–46	Text of play, lacking at least three leaves, including an initial leaf or leaves, containing the title and the start of the text, and leaves 14 and 16, which have been removed, leaving tiny stubs.
47	Blank.
48–9	Rough notes on legal business relating to rents and tenure of lands, headed 'Poynts to be observed by my fathers directions'.
50a	A few lines, headed 'i6i6 Merthines Prophysyes translated'.
50b	Itemised payments for 'strabeeres' (strawberries).
51a	A few lines, headed 'i6i9 Merthines destinies translated'.
51b	Draft of verses, beginning 'such is the force of Beuty'.
52–6	Removed, leaving small stubs.
57–8a	Blank.
58b	Transcript of verses, beginning 'when she is angry'.
59	Removed, leaving stub.
60–1a	Transcript of verses, beginning 'Fayere yonge man be content'.
61b	Memorandum relating to a tenancy, dated 8 September 1619.
62a	Blank.
62b	Transcript of verses in Welsh, beginning 'Oer ddig pob musig'.
63a	Transcript of verses in Welsh, beginning 'rwv j yn drwm am adel'.
63b	Inventory of books and other items, headed 'A briefe of my bookes'.
64a	Blank.
64b	Columns of figures, pen tests and other scribbles.

The manuscript is made up of nine gatherings in quarto, each now separately mounted, so that conjugacy of leaves is clearly visible, although Fols. 13–19 have been separated from their conjugate partners. The leaves measure 150 mm × 185–190 mm. There is no sign of trimming, although there has been some loss through crumbling at the edges (e.g. Fol. 1) and corners (e.g. Fol. 41). Blotting on 46b and 47a suggests that after the transcript was made no intervening leaves were removed. Damp stains in the inner margin of Fol. 1 are not visible in Fol. 2, and patterns of blotting do not correspond between 17b and 18a, 43b and 44a, and 44b and 45a.

The irregularities in gatherings 1, 2, 6, 8, and 9 may reflect no more than the use of the missing folds for other purposes after the sheets were folded and cut, but before they were gathered and bound. However, the incomplete gatherings 1 and 8 may well be the surviving leaves from the folds missing from gatherings 2 and 6. The absence of one or more leaves from the beginning of the play may be accounted for by the usual vulnerability of the outer leaves of a much handled manuscript, but Fols. 14 and 16 must have been deliberately removed after the play was copied. It is tempting to conjecture that their disappearance may be due to disapproval of their contents, which must have included the unhorsing of King Arthur by the Red Rose Knight at a tournament and the Knight's invasion of France. Missing leaves later in the manuscript may have been blank: their removal has not affected the remaining entries in the book. Irregularity in the size of the gatherings does not seem to be significant: in the play text a change of hand only once coincides with the start of a new gathering (Fol. 36a). The make-up of the manuscript, and incidence of watermarks are:

Gathering	*Folio*	*Watermark*	*Description*
1	[ ].1	w	One sheet or half-sheet: lacks one or three leaves
2	2.11	w	Three sheets folded inside each other: lacks one watermarked fold (? gathering 1) conjugate with Fols. 6–7
	3.10	–	
	4.9	w	
	5.8	–	
	6.7	–	
3	12.19	–	Two sheets folded inside each other: Fols. 14, 16 removed
	13.18	w	
	[14].17	–	
	15.[16]	w	
4	20.35	w	Four sheets folded inside each other
	21.34	–	
	22.33	–	
	23.32	w	
	24.31	w	
	25.30	–	
	26.29	–	
	27.28	w	
5	36.43	w	Two sheets folded inside each other
	37.42	–	
	38.41	w	
	39.40	–	
6	44.49	w	Two sheets folded inside each other: lacks unwatermarked fold conjugate with Fols. 44.49
	45.48	w	
	46.47	–	
7	50.57	–	Two sheets folded inside each other, Fols. 52–6 removed
	51.[56]	w	
	[52.55]		
	[53.54]		
8	58.[65]	–	Single sheet, lacks watermarked fold and unwatermarked leaf conjugate with Fol. 58
9	[59].64	–	Two sheets: lacks watermarked fold conjugate with Fols. 61–2
	60.63	w	
	61.62	–	

Hands and Transcription of the Play

The play text, which occupies the first 46 folios, is a transcript in five different hands, two of which make only the briefest of appearances. The transcription of the play is divided among the hands as follows:

Folio	*Line Numbers*	*Hand*	*Number of Lines Transcribed*	*Plates*
1–4b	1–253	A	253	
4b–5a	254–64	B	9½	Plate 5 (259–68)
5a–b	264–318	A	54½	
6a–7b	319–424	C	105½	
7b–8b	424–92	A	68	Plate 8 (482–502)
8b–9b	492–573	C	82½	
10a–12b	574–742	A	169	
12b–13b	743–831	D	89	
14	Missing			
15a	832–3	A	2	
15a	834–68	D	35	
15b	869–910	A	42	
16	911–14 (fragment)	A	4	
17a–21b	915–1283	A	368½	
21b	1283–90	E	7½	Plate 2 (1109–45)
21b–24a	1291–1474	A	183½	Plate 6 (1282–93)
24a	1474–93	D	19½	Plate 9 (1463–83)
24b–27a	1494–1680	C	187	Plate 3 (1561–93)
27a–29b	1681–1855	A	175	
29b	1856–71	D	16	Plate 10 (1855–90)
29b	1872–79	C	8	
29b–30a	1880–1927	D	48	
30b–31a	1928–92	C	65	
31b–32b	1993–2078	A	86	Plate 1 (2032–70)
32b–33b	2079–2170	C	92	
34a–b	2171–2243	D	73	
35a–b	2244–2317	C	74	
36a–b	2318–91	D	74	Plate 4 (2318–54)
37a	2392–2427	C	36	
37b–38b	2428–2532	A	105	
39a–b	2533–2605	D	73	
40a–41a	2606–2704	C	99	
41b	2705–39	A	35	
42a–43a	2740–2845	D	106	
43b–44a	2846–2906	C	61	
44a	2907–17	D	11	
44b	2918–33	C	16	
44b–46b	2934–3095	A	162	Plate 7 (3091–5)

The shares of the copyists differ radically: A writes 1707½ lines, B 9½, C 826, D 544½, and E a mere 7½. The alternating stints of the three principal scribes and the presence of the other two may suggest that the copying was done under pressure of time and that continuous transcription was a high priority. The evidence for this is strongest where C takes over from D for eight lines in the middle of Fol. 29b (ll.1872–9: see Plate 10). All the copyists of the play use secretary hands with some mixture of italic letter forms. B and E hardly had time to warm to the task and both accordingly seem stiff and formal (Plates 5, 6).

The remaining items in the manuscript are in two or more hands: all but those on Fols. 60–1a (Plate 14) and, perhaps, Fol. 51b (Plate 13), could imaginably be Hand A of the play text, which is remarkable for its variations in size, neatness and cursiveness (Plates 1, 2, 5–10). The hand which transcribes the verses on Fols. 60–1a bears no resemblance to any other in the manuscript (see below, p. xxxv).

Hand A is apparently the 'Morganus: Evans:' whose name is subscribed at the end of the play. This is a quirky and fussy hand which shows a greater range of variation than any of the others. A's pages vary in length from 27 to 42 lines, with a norm, once he has settled down, of 35–7 lines. A is careful with the layout of his pages, indenting verse and highlighting stage directions either by increasing the size of his letters and using large italic forms (as also sometimes for proper names within the text), or by enclosing them in prominent square brackets or box rules (see Plates 1 and 2). The slope of his lines can tend steeply downwards when he is under pressure (for example Fols. 45b–46a). At several points in his work he seems to trim his pen or resume work after a break (for example, at ll. 302, 721, 894, 923, 962, and 1348), but there are no noticeable changes in the ink (the same supply appears to have been used by all the scribes). A's markedly smaller writing for some prose passages seems to result from a conscious decision (most clearly on Fol. 45a, but see also Plate 1). He is freer than C and D in his use of abbreviations, making regular use of an upwards clockwise loop for *er*, two forms of ampersand, distinct forms for *pre*, *per*/*par* and *pro* (see Plate 2: ll. 1117, 1123, 1132), tildes for *m*, *n* and *cion*, and twice adopting the 9-formed suspension for final *us* (441 and 2991: also used once by Hand E (Plate 6: l. 1285), but not by the others). His habitual formation of final *s* is similar to the common abbreviation for *es*/*is*, but his use of it in such words as *thus*, *yes*, *was* and Latin words ending in *us* makes it clear that he cannot intend the abbreviation (Plates 1, 2, 8, and 9). He has a habit of writing *rr* where *ir* is required, and of correcting himself by dotting the first *r* (for example, ll. 906 *thirty*, 1079 *firm*, 2730 *fire*).

A has a number of fairly consistent, distinctive spellings, among them *doe*, *goe*, *noe*, *soe*, *whoe*, *whome*, *woeman*; *on* (one), *non*; *dy*, *ly*, *ey* (eye); *yt* (it); *ould*, *bould*, *tould*. More idiosyncratic are *desiere*, *miery* (merry), *pitiefull*, *revievd*, *siely* (silly), *wiefe*, and especially *salph*(*ly*) and its variant *salfe* (safe).

Hand C stands in the strongest contrast to A (see Plates 3 and 8). Where

A is fussy and variable, given to decoration and elaboration of letter forms, especially majuscules, C is cursive, confident and consistent. His pages present the reader with the greatest initial difficulty of all the hands, because he frequently leaves his letter forms uncompleted. Closer acquaintance with the hand leaves relatively few difficulties of transcription, because the context usually determines whether, for instance, a given form is meant for *h* or *th*, *te* or *to*, *sl* or *ft*. More troublesome is his habit of completing final *c* or *g* with a flourish in such a manner as to leave doubt whether he intends a following *e*: many of these are represented in this edition as ^{e}. C's minuscules show a preference for secretary forms, except for *h* and *r*. His majuscules are less regular, and he uses alternative forms of several letters, *A*, *C*, *E*, *G*, *H*, *M*, and *P* among them. His initial secretary *d* varies in size, and may sometimes be intended as a majuscule. In the majority of instances, however, this seems unlikely, and this edition prints all but a very few (where the intention to capitalize is unequivocal; for example, l. 1584 *Dido*: see Plate 3) as minuscules, reserving the majuscule for his alternative form of *D*. Difficulty can arise from C's tendency to leave *t* uncrossed and to write *tt* as *ll*. His superscript *u* and *r* are hard to distinguish from each other in *yo*^{u} and *yo*^{r}. Like A he makes regular use of abbreviations, especially a final upward anticlockwise loop for *er* and the distinctive *p* with a looped tail for *per*/*par*. He also makes free use of the tilde for nasal consonants and almost invariably uses a simple looped ampersand. He differs from A in avoiding the abbreviations for *pro-* and *-us*. His characteristic spellings include *ame*, *one* (on), and *furth*.

C's pages are immediately recognizable from the strong upward slant of his lines and a tendency for the left margin to creep further left as he moves down the page. Stage directions in the right margin are sometimes distinguished by brackets or slashes, but more often by a long dash. Verse and songs are distinguished by indentation. The number of lines in C's pages varies between 29 and 36. From Fol. 32b onwards, C approaches near-illegibility, particularly on Fols. 40a and 41a: this is presumably because he was attempting to copy his text more quickly. The final line of Fol. 33b is squeezed in so as to suggest that the scribes were working strictly to stints consisting of whole pages, a practice which might have permitted them to work simultaneously. Similar crowding is found in some pages of A's and D's work.

D is the most distinctive of the three main hands (see Plates 4, 9 and 10). His hand is small, neat and very regular in its secretary letter forms, apart from a few variant majuscules. His layout is tidy and consistent, although even he gives evidence of working under pressure of time in his later pages (for example Fol. 34a). He places a brace or, occasionally, an opening parenthesis before stage directions in the right margin, and he makes use of initial " for extended quotation (where A and C employ 《). Difficulties in reading Hand D can arise from his use of a single form for either *h* or long *s* (see, for example, l. 2326 *soone*, *salue*, *sore*, *how*: Plate 4), but otherwise the hand is clear and legible, despite a greater tendency than either A or C to decorate his text with initial and final flourishes. His favourite form of abbreviation is the tilde, which can, when final, be elegantly flourished: he also abbreviates *per/par*. Unlike the other scribes, he abbreviates *er* only after *p* and makes no use of the ampersand. D and C both abbreviate the word *letter* as *lr̄e* in neighbouring scenes (lines 2756, 2757, 2763 (D) and 2876 (C)): this coincidence may indicate the preservation of a form in the copy. D's characteristic spellings include *freind*(*s*), and the use of *dg* in such words as *liedge*, *siedge*, and *chardge*.

D's pages generally contain from 34 to 36 lines, although he does drop to 33 and rise to 39. His work is sometimes crowded towards the end of the page, notably on Fol. 44a, where three lines of verse are squeezed into two text lines. At the foot of Fol. 42a the phrase 'thy happie ship past by' (l. 2776) appears to have been added in a gap left for it. In common with A and C, Hand D is given to placing speech prefixes higher than the line to which they refer.

Of hands B and E it must suffice to say that B is an upright hand, clear in the linking of letters and the division of words, with heavy descenders and a tendency to flourish *d*, *g*, and *v*; while E is neat, square and spiky, punctuates heavily, and is characterized by strong diagonal hairlines for initial *v*, *m*, and *I* (see Plates 5 and 6).

The pattern of alternation of the principal hands indicates five main phases of work:

Stint	Hands		Lines
1i	A (with B)	:	lines 1–318 (Fols. 1a–5b)
ii	A and C	:	lines 319–742 (Fols. 6a–12b)
2	A and D (with E)	:	lines 743–1474 (Fols. 12b–24a)
3	A, C and D	:	lines 1474–2078 (Fols. 24a–32b)
4	C and D	:	lines 2079–2427 (Fols. 32b–37a)
5i	A, C and D	:	lines 2428–2933 (Fols. 37b–44b)
ii	A	:	lines 2934–3095 (Fols. 44b–46b)

Two conclusions seem incontestable: each of the main scribes was allowed one substantial rest in the course of the work (stints 1 (D), 2 (C) and 4 (A)); and A, who copied more than half of the play, including the ending (and presumably the lost opening), had the largest stake in the enterprise. Three questions remain to which only tentative answers can be offered: do the three main scribes vary much in reliability? what can their practice tell us of the nature of their exemplar? was any copyist also author or part-author of the play?

Assuming that the underlying copy was accurate and reasonably consistent, on the evidence of certain or probable error, A was least reliable in respect of omission and misplacing of stage directions, omitting at least 27 and misplacing a further 28 (comparative figures for C are 9 and 7, and for D 9 and 4). D was the most inclined of the three main scribes to omit words or short phrases

(D 9: C 9; A 11). D also twice converts a plural Latin stage direction into the singular, against once each for A and C, with their longer stints. Other categories of error more nearly reflect the proportion of their shares in the job: verse was mislined nine times by A, six by C and twice by D; A omitted eight speech prefixes, C five and D none. Their rates for other categories of error (radical misspelling etc.) are: A 29 or more; C 19 and D 13—a high proportional rate for D.

The exemplar from which the scribes worked appears to have been a tidy copy of the play, well equipped with stage directions. A's emphatic boxing of stage directions might seem to reflect a similarly professional layout in the exemplar, were it not for C's and D's divergent practice. One orthographic oddity which perhaps reflects copy is the spelling, shared by all three scribes, of several words with an *o* where *a* might have been expected, notably the name *Mob*, but likewise *Goffer*, for the more familiar *Gaffer*. It is unclear whether they were repeating a common error caused by the hand of their original, or were accurately transmitting its preferred spelling of these words. The most interesting unusual spelling occurs at l. 2123, where C has spelled the affirmative interjection *aye* as *eye*. The usual spelling of the word in the early seventeenth century was *I*. However, one prolific author, the dramatist, pamphleteer, and poet, Thomas Heywood, made regular use of the spelling *ey*, to the frequent confusion of compositors setting his works, who easily mistook it for the noun or verb *eye*. Although the *OED* lists the form *ey* as current from the seventeenth to the nineteenth century, its only early example is from Heywood's *Royal King and Loyal Subject* (1637). The form occurs in his autograph manuscripts. It is also to be found, more or less frequently in relation to compositorial tolerance of it, in most of his printed plays.[9] C's use of a rare minority spelling may itself be the result of some such confusion—the more so as the passage in question is one of the play's many mad speeches. It may also be significant that A at first wrote *I*, before substituting the correct *eie* at l. 1253.

All the principal copyists were prone to errors of normal and expected kinds. Were any of them author or part-author of the play, one might expect to find occasional corrections, or even minor revisions, of the text. None of the *currente calamo* corrections with which the transcript abounds falls clearly into either category, error or revision, apart from the possible addition of two stage directions in a hand other than that of the current scribe (ll. 122, and 2331: see Plate 4). This implies, at most, that one scribe (perhaps C) glanced through the work of the others and happened to spot two stray omissions among many unnoticed ones. Given the possibility that A may have composed at least part of the play,

[9] See A. Brown, 'An Edition of the Plays of Thomas Heywood', *Renaissance Papers* (1954), 71–6; 'Two Notes on Thomas Heywood: I. A spelling of Heywood's', *Modern Language Review*, 50 (1955), 497–8; W. W. Greg, *Collected Papers* , ed. J. C. Maxwell (Oxford 1966), p. 160 n. 1.

these findings are unexpected, although his participation in writing the play need not be entirely ruled out by them. The evident pressure of time on the process of copying may have inhibited creative thought and increased the normal tendency of an unprofessional scribe towards inadvertent error.

If the conjecture of an exemplar in the hand of Heywood were entertained, the marked frequency of false starts and minor corrections in the transcript would at once become more intelligible. Like Hand C in the transcript (which it resembles in general character, but with which it is certainly not identical), Heywood's hand is perfectly legible, with practice, but its extreme cursiveness can cause great trouble until one becomes thoroughly familiar with it.[10]

The Play

Date, Sources, and Treatment

Memoranda in the latter part of the manuscript include three dated items, which afford a plausible *terminus ad quem* for the transcription, and thus the composition of the play. Short beginnings of translations from 'Merthines Prophysyes' and 'Merthines destinies' for 1616 and 1619 respectively appear on Fols. 50a and 51a, and on Fol. 61b there is a memorandum about a tenancy, dated 8 September 1619. It is reasonable to assume that the play was transcribed before 1616, and that the remaining portion of the manuscript book was used later. The *terminus a quo* for composition is fixed firmly as 1607 by the author's knowledge of the second part of Richard Johnson's romance, first printed in that year. What appear to be allusions to *The Winter's Tale*, *The Tempest*, and perhaps *Cymbeline* would advance the date to around 1611.

Since the play is largely based on the prose romance *Tom a Lincoln*, it seems appropriate to attach to it the same title. By 1611, that name already had several associations. Its primary reference was to the great bell of Lincoln Cathedral, which gained topicality when the bell was recast on 3 December 1610 and rehung on 27 January 1611.[11] The name may also have been given to a famous fighting bear in the Bear Gardens, to which—rather than to the bell—Thomas Nashe may refer in 1592 in the phrase 'thou shouldst heare Tom a Lincolne roare'. However, the clearest evidence for the naming of the bear dates from as late as 1677.[12]

[10] See the texts and introductions of the Malone Society Reprints of *The Captives*, ed. A. Brown (Oxford, 1953) and *The Escapes of Jupiter*, ed. H. D. Janzen (Oxford, 1976).

[11] B. Maxwell, *Studies in Beaumont, Fletcher, and Massinger* (Chapel Hill, 1939), pp. 35–6.

[12] See Sir S. Lee, 'Bearbaiting, Bullbaiting, and Cockfighting', in *Shakespeare's England*, ed. C. T. Onions, 2 vols. (Oxford, 1917), ii. 432; J. Simons, 'A Possible Elucidation of an Obscure References [*sic*] in Nashe's *Four Letters Confuted*', *Notes & Queries*, 226 (1981), 521: *The Works of Thomas Nashe*, ed. R. B. Mckerrow, 5 vols. (1904–10; 1958), i. 321.

The two parts of 'The most pleasant History of TOM A LINCOLNE, That renowned Souldier, the RED-ROSE Knight, who for his Valour and Chivalry, was surnamed *The Boast of England*', by R.I., may have appeared in print in 1598–9 and 1607 respectively.[13] The 'R.I.' to whom it is attributed was Richard Johnson, a versatile and productive popular writer who flourished between 1591 and 1621. The earliest surviving edition of the romance describes itself as '*The sixth impression*' and is dated 1631. Like all later reprints, of which six are known with dates from 1635 to 1704, this edition contains both parts.

The romance, although fairly short, is episodic, depending for its effect more on variety of matter than ingenuity of plotting. Broadly speaking, the seven chapters of Part 1 bring Tom from birth, as the bastard son of King Arthur and a court lady called Angelica, through a humble childhood as supposed son of a shepherd near Lincoln (site of the monastery which conceals Arthur's clandestine amour, a clear derivative from the story of Henry II and fair Rosamund), to his highest point of fortune, marriage to Anglitora, daughter of Prester John. The events of Part 1 leave Tom twice a father. By Caelia, Queen of Fairyland (a figure of deserted love based on Ovidian heroines such as Phyllis and Dido), he has a son, whose adventures, as the Fairy Knight, occupy the eighth and last chapter of Part 2. By Anglitora, he has a second son, The Black Knight. Part 1 ends with Tom still blissfully ignorant of the identity of his father and mother. Part 2 starts with Arthur's injudicious deathbed confession of his delinquency. Mayhem ensues: the widowed Queen exacts gruesome vengeance on Angelica, and Anglitora, scorning her base-born husband, decamps with her son to live in foreign parts as an adulteress. Tom's miseries end in his death at the hands of Anglitora, whose own death follows soon after when she is murdered by her son. Almost as an afterthought, the romance concludes with the affecting friendship of the half-brothers, the Black Knight and the Fairy Knight, who end their days in Lincoln, where they build 'a most sumptuous Minster, which to this day remaines in great magnificence and glory'.[14] Needless to say, the great bell of Lincoln Cathedral figures in Part 1 as Tom's lavish gift to the funeral solemnities of his rural foster-father, dead of grief at his son's desertion to become a robber on Barnsdale Heath.[15]

For all his evident knowledge of Part 2—apparent from the very first page,

[13] These dates are based on the evidence of entries in the Stationers' Register, 24 December 1599 and 20 October 1607: see *R.I., The Most Pleasant History of Tom a Lincolne*, ed. Richard S. M. Hirsch (Columbia, South Carolina, 1978), p. xix.

[14] Quoted from Hirsch, p. 94.

[15] This is a location in south Yorkshire, which aptly associates Tom with the tradition of Robin Hood, but sorts oddly with his taking of the red rose as his personal emblem. A map in R. B. Dobson and J. Taylor, *Rymes of Robyn Hood* (London, 1976), p. 69, shows Barnsdale as the area between the rivers Went and Don, between Barnsley to the west, Wentbridge to the north, and Doncaster to the south.

where Angelica anticipates the murderous rage of Guinivere (ll. 22–3)—the author of the play bases its action entirely on the events of Part 1 of Johnson's romance. Only twice does the play diverge from those events. (1) The Portuguese expedition described in Chapter III becomes in the play an invasion of France (a provocative topic, and one which offered opportunities for frequent allusion to Shakespeare's Falstaff plays). It is this episode which is affected by the loss of Fols. 14 and 16, so that its significance remains slightly obscure, although reference is made to it later at l. 2931. (2) The play makes no use of the interpolated narrative of Valentine and Dulcippa used by Johnson to pad out Chapter V (a narrative which has its own interest as an analogue of the wager plot in *Cymbeline*).

The principal episodes of Johnson's romance are used in the play to sustain a great variety of material which has little or nothing to do with them. The comic matter, amounting to about a third of the play, is entirely the dramatist's invention. This centres on Tom's clownish follower Rusticano (whose name may be related to the 'Markasius Rusticanus' mentioned in the printed text of *Gesta Grayorum* (1594)).[16] It also includes a scene for the four old shepherds who are the fathers of Tom's group of childhood friends and whose classical names bring a whiff of pastoral into Lincolnshire (ll. 314–403). Many minor characters, among them Queen Guinivere (who makes her first appearance in the romance in Part 2), Sir Lancelot and Sir Tristram, seem to owe their place in the play mainly to their utility as butts for the clown's jokes. Rusticano's role contains a generous provision of set speeches as well as many dialogues of verbal mistaking, proverb-chopping or social and linguistic cross-purposes. He is, by turns, salacious, mock-heroic, greedy, drunk, hungry—he even has a parody of Jacobean sermon rhetoric (ll. 1295–1304), a sleep-walking scene in which he imagines himself to be dead (ll. 1474–93), and a sleepy early-morning entry 'wth one hose of the other one, wthout any brichis' (ll. 2418–19).

The chorus, Time, is a further addition. He is a figure who combines the emblematic person of Time, as used in *The Winter's Tale* and other plays, with functions which more closely resemble those of Gower in *Pericles*, or Homer in Heywood's sequence of plays about the *Ages*. His opening speech, for which there is no counterpart in Johnson, conveys the distinctive tone of the play (ll. 123–35):

> I that have bene ere since the world began
> I that was[e] since this orbed balls creation
> I that have seen huge kingedomes devastācons
> Doe heare ꝑsent my selfe to yor still viwve
> Ould, aunciant, changinge, eu*er* runninge time
> first clad in gowld, next silver, next that brasse

[16] Malone Society Reprint, ed. W. W. Greg (Oxford, 1914), p. 13, l. 19.

And nowe in Iron, Inferiour to the rest
and yet more heard then all/ & soe ye times are now⟨e⟩
Noe marvayle then/ the times are Irō/ mē scarce demd m̅e̅
what cannot learnings arte effectuat
time longe since gone, & past yt now calls backe
to tell a story of a princely knight
his birth & fortunes noe lesse strange [and] then rare

Croft quoted this passage as evidence for the dramatist's knowledge of *The Winter's Tale*, which, indeed, it may well be, especially since the speech goes on to specify a time-gap of sixteen years between Tom's birth and his entry into the action, of which Johnson makes no mention. Equally noteworthy, however, is the extended reference to the four ages, after which Heywood named five of his plays within a few years on either side of 1610. The ages receive comparable extended treatment in the prologue to the third of them, *The Brazen Age* (printed 1613).

Although the author confined his action to the events of Part 1 of Johnson's romance, he knew Part 2 as well, and he used the knowledge in one scene where he chose to alter the narrative. In both works, Anglitora, daughter of Prester John, elopes with Tom in the clear conviction that her father will not allow her to marry him. In the romance, Prester John has previously refused his consent (although Tom has duly won her hand as the prize proposed for killing a dragon), claiming that 'first hee would loose his Kingdome, before shee should bee the wife of a wandering Knight'. The lovers elope—prematurely, it turns out, as Prester John, having slept on it, is upset by his rudeness to Tom and changes his mind. He finds in the morning that his guest has vanished and that his daughter's chamber is empty, leaving him to face 'nothing but relentlesse walles, which in vaine hee might speake vnto'.[17] He laments for many days, but eventually gets over it. The play handles this episode differently. Anglitora, knowing that her father has vowed never to marry her to a foreigner, elopes without consulting him, contrary to her own stated principle (ll. 2368–71):

if men affect yo^{u} and yo^{u} them the like
if freinds do not consent the match vp strike
yet first entreate them to consent thereto
see if they will, if not wed, bed, and [doe] wooe

Prester John's reaction likewise differs. On learning of their flight, he curses Tom and Anglitora, reaching a climax with ll. 2580–924, in which he prophesies the eventual death of Tom at the hands of Anglitora. Echoes of *King Lear* here and of *Hamlet* later in the scene reveal how far Johnson's romance is from being

[17] Hirsch, p. 49.

the sole source of the play. It is pervaded with reminiscence, of Shakespeare, of Heywood and of other writers, ancient and modern, Ovid and Spenser among them.

The hectic intensity of Prester John's passion would be prime evidence in any attempt to argue that the play of *Tom a Lincoln* is directly parodic. Such intentions would certainly go far to account for the reshaping of the romance narrative in this episode. In the play, but not in the romance, Prester John is supplied with a queen, called Bellamy. She responds to the elopement by running mad (as her daughter had done in the previous scene, mistakenly supposing Tom to have succumbed to the dragon, where Johnson had accounted for her passion more reasonably as fear about the result of the coming encounter). Bellamy's suicide soon follows and this is reported to the king by a lord (to whom the fates of Lear and Ophelia are no secret):

> My liege I bring you sole sad newes the queene
> distract & senceles ran orethwart the meades
> decking her head with cockle, fearne-locke tares
> that growe dispersed one the Campion plaine
> mixt teares wth smiles shee ecchoes furth this note
> as burthen to her swanlike mourne full song
> my daughter sweet Ang: is gone
> and to a swift-hed torrent comes at last
> wherein shee casts her self. oh not her self
> her garments bare her one the silu*er* streame
> meane while shee senceles of her misery
> sate warbling furth the pleasantst notes shee could
> ere helpe could succur her shee layed her head
> vpon the riu*er*s bosome sanke & dyed.
>
> (ll. 2647–60)

Next for suicide is Prester John himself: he takes longer about it, and the matter of his dying speech (ll. 2661–88) seems to be indebted to a suicidal speech by the Black Knight in Part 2 of the romance.[18]

What the play does is to convert the comitragic pattern of Johnson's two-part romance into a version of the events of Part 1: this is made tragicomic by the simple expedient of piling up horrors towards a happy resolution. In both romance and play the marriage of Tom and Anglitora entails the suicide of Caelia, the Fairy Queen, who has a prior claim on Tom: the play adds the deaths of Prester John and Bellamy. The transition to a comic ending after these deaths is effected with shameless facility by a final use of the chorus (see ll. 2847–60).

There are signs at the end of the play that a sequel may have been intended,

[18] Hirsch, pp. 91–2.

or at least left in prospect.[19] Tom is still ignorant of his parentage and of his fathering of the Fairy Knight; an ominous note is sounded by the song which accompanies the final wedding procession. After four stanzas of celebration, it ends (ll. 3054–61):

Braue Arthur thow dost know thy sonne
wich ioyes thee much though thow Conceale yt
but yet before thy glasses runne
to his great griefe thou wilt reveale yt

but peace vayne tongue that bablst soe
yt nought befitts this sacred mirth
goe one, goe one, & as they goe
be ioyfull heaven be frolicke earth

In the manuscript, the last stanza is separated from the others by a horizontal line, suggesting perhaps an intention to omit it on some occasion of performance. Certainly these two stanzas seem strangely at odds with the spirit of festivity at the end of the surviving text of the play.

In summary, one may say of the play's adaptation of its source that a passive, almost slavish, following of the main events of the romance goes hand in hand with a radical shift in tone, most apparent in the emphasis given to the clown. This may well reflect the assumed taste of an audience quite unlike the literate female readership at which Johnson's romance would appear to be directed. The play seems to envisage a predominantly male audience, perhaps with a preponderance of younger members. Its self-parodying heroics, smart cynicism and adolescent sexual humour are not at all difficult to reconcile with the notion that *Tom a Lincoln* was written as a Christmas entertainment for one of the Inns of Court.

Performance and Context

All the signs are that the manuscript was prepared by amateurs rather than people connected with the professional theatre. Yet the play it preserves shows at least the formal features of professional work. It is long: the 3095 lines of the diplomatic transcript expand to over 3400 in a modernised edited text, when Hand D's packed pages are relined. Three or more missing leaves imply the loss of not less than a further 200 lines of text. The staging of the play requires a curtained space with a bed behind the curtain, and possibly also a practicable 'rock' for Caelia to throw herself off, demands which might be differently

[19] A play or masque called *The Fairy Knight*, by Dekker and Ford, was licensed 11 June 1624. The text has not survived, and it would be unwise to associate either of these writers with *Tom a Lincoln*, or its possible sequel, on this evidence alone.

catered for on private and public occasions. One feature of the text which would be unexpected in a professional play of the years after 1605 is the proliferation of oaths. A small but possibly significant pointer to indoor performance is the reference (l. 1718) to the audience as seated.

Analysis of the casting requirements reveals a professional economy. The play's many roles are deployed so that it can be performed by a cast of eleven men and five boys—something like the norm for a professional company in the second decade of the seventeenth century. An action consisting of eighteen or nineteen scenes (depending on how much was lost by the removal of Fols. 14 and 16) again suggests normal dramaturgy for the period and for the type of play, as does the expedient of using five choric speeches to paste over the gaps in an episodic action.

The play's stage directions, which use the formulae of the professional playhouses, are extended and circumstantial. Consider, for example (ll. 165–71, 1968–9, 2031):

> A Dumbe shew
> Enter the Abbesse in hast wth the infant in her arms & kissinge yt
> she layes yt downe standing a farre of, enter an ould sheapheard
> whoe espyinge the babe takes yt vp greatly reioicinge, & exit, wich
> don, the Abbesse wth much ioy dep*ar*teth, then time discou*er*s Angell:
> In her bed awake, weepinge & lamentinge, wth the kinge
> strivinge to comfort her, wch done time[s] drawes ye curtayne speakinge as before
>
> Enter Cælia. her hayre hanging carelesly wth her babe
> [hanging care] in her armes, & 2 ladyes &c.
>
> Exeunt: Cæ: at one dore, La: at another

Stage directions are generally adequate: very few which are not clearly implied by the text are missing. There is evidence of confusion about the details of action during the French military scenes (ll. 939–41) but only one passage involves radical inconsistency. This occurs on Fol. 7b, where the clown, Rusticano, has a 23-line speech (ll. 422–44) apparently designed to cover offstage action by other characters, after which he carries on (without either a break or a re-entry direction for the other speakers), to describe his own involvement in that same action. The clown's speech, which is irrelevant to the context and wholly self-contained, may have been added without a full understanding that it was inconsistent with the accompanying and following action. Nothing in the physical makeup of the manuscript between Fols. 7 and 8 indicates a hiatus in the text. If a hiatus is indeed the cause of the inconsistency (as the absence of an entry direction might imply) then it must have occurred in the exemplar rather than the copy. Another explanation might be that A for some reason skipped a passage while working on the end of Fol. 7b and the start of Fol. 8a which contained the text and direction needed to resolve this difficulty.

The role of Rusticano includes several other soliloquies which could equally well be omitted without impairing the action. The quality and dominance of his part, which rivals even Tom's, may in itself be evidence that the play was connected with a professional company. It is conceivable that the role was augmented for a particular performance, and even that it was written with a professional clown in mind.[20] Certainly Rusticano's function as Tom's most faithful follower, companion and fool ensures his presence throughout, and his racy and salacious prose is a welcome relief from the play's generally undistinguished verse. His is the only role for which no hint is to be found in Johnson's romance.

The discovery of *Tom a Lincoln* adds a third to the plays known to have been based on Johnson's writings. The other two are Thomas Heywood's *The Four Prentices of London* (written ?1592–1600, printed in 1632), which makes limited use of Johnson's *The Nine Worthies of London* (1592); and *The Seven Champions of Christendom* (printed in 1638), which dramatizes episodes from Johnson's highly popular romance of the same name, whose two parts were first printed in 1596 and 1597. Its author, like the author of *Tom a Lincoln*, invented a major role for a clown, through which to link and unify the episodes of a straggling action.[21] John Kirke to whom, on the strength of the initials 'I.K.', *The Seven Champions* is customarily assigned, is an obscure figure, known only in the 1630s and early 1640s: his role in the publication of a handful of plays may have been that of supplier of copy rather than author. Thomas Heywood's participation in the writing of *The Seven Champions* has also been proposed, together with a date for its composition of 1613–14.[22] These two plays, *The Four Prentices* and *The Seven Champions*, and a number like them, including *Guy of Warwick* ('by B.J.') and *The Thracian Wonder* (attributed to Webster and Rowley), testify to the survival of a taste for half-serious and undemanding romantic drama. It is with such plays that *Tom a Lincoln* should in some respects be aligned.

Two main possibilites emerge. One is that *Tom a Lincoln*, by a professional writer or writers, belonged to the repertoire of a professional company but was adapted for the special conditions of a Christmas performance at Gray's Inn.

[20] See Bradbrook, 'A New Jacobean Play', p. 5. In 'Shakespeare and the Multiple Theatres', in G. R. Hibbard (ed.), *Elizabeth Theatre* vi (1978), p. 99 n. 15, Professor Bradbrook again argues for a connection between Rusticano, the Red Bull playhouse and its clown Thomas Greene.

[21] See J. Kirke, *The Seven Champions of Christendom (1638)*, ed. G. E. Dawson (Cleveland, Ohio, 1929), pp. xiv–xv.

[22] See Paul Merchant, 'Thomas Heywood's hand in *The Seven Champions of Christendom*', 5, *The Library*, 33 (1978), 226–30. Merchant finds reason to take seriously the date 1613–14 proposed for the romance by John Freehafer, 'Shakespeare's *Tempest* and *The Seven Champions*', *Studies in Philology*, 66 (1969), 87–103.

The other, perhaps more likely, is that the play was written expressly for the Gray's Inn Christmas revels, though whether by students with an extensive knowledge of current theatre or by a professional engaged by them must remain an open question. On the first hypothesis, the evident haste with which the surviving text was copied might be explained by the need to return the exemplar to its owners quickly. On the second, that haste might be motivated by shortage of time in which to submit a copy to the seniors of the Inn for their approval before performance.

Tom a Lincoln and Shakespeare

It is hardly surprising that one of the first things which caught the attention of the scholars who discovered *Tom a Lincoln* was the pervasive presence of allusions to, or echoes of, Shakespeare. These cover a wide range of plays and extend from stray verbal debts such as 'night-tripping fairies' (l. 201; *Henry IV*, I.i.87), to the more extended reminiscences of *Hamlet*, *King Lear*, and *The Winter's Tale* pointed to above. Croft may have overstated the debt to *The Winter's Tale*: the farcical disguises and absurd prophecy which effect the denouement are at least as likely to poke fun at *Cymbeline*.

The character of *Tom a Lincoln* as parody, or as an instance of a loose-knit romantic play with an old-fashioned episodic plot and a dominant clown, associates it with the years after 1608 when such plays made a notable comeback on the London stage. It also distinguishes it from Shakespeare's intention and achievement in transmuting this generic pattern into plays of wide sympathy and deep feeling. Its very structure may, accordingly, be influenced by mockery of that generic pattern, and consequently of Shakespeare's plays as well as every one else's. What seems to be more distinctive is the presence of what may be identified as specific echoes of Shakespeare's words. Here direct influence or parodic intent is harder to demonstrate: the author of *Tom a Lincoln* was of a generation which reflected, often unconsciously, the difficulty of following Shakespeare's achievement. Heywood's plays frequently show him using a Shakespearean locution where one need suspect neither parody nor even a full consciousness of what he was doing. It is also, of course, not unlikely that modern academic readers, more widely read in Shakespeare than in all the other drama of the period, will identify an echo of his work, but miss traces of other writers.

A short selective list may draw attention to the range and variety of the Shakespearean echoes noted so far. If these really are reminiscences of Shakespeare's plays, rather than instances of the common idiom and linguistic currency of the time, they offer striking testimony to the memorability of those plays (either in performance or in the early quartos).

Line reference in *Tom a Lincoln*	Shakespeare (Riverside lines)
83	*Hamlet*, III.i.55
123	*Winter's Tale*, IV.i.10–11
201	*1 Henry IV*, I.i.87
341–2	*Winter's Tale*, I.ii.37
544	*Romeo & Juliet*, V.i.24
545 ff.	*Lear, passim*
950–4	*1 Henry IV*, V.iv.121–9
1445, 1606	*Lear*, III.vi.109
2000	*Lear*, V.iii.258
2264	*Antony & Cleopatra*, IV.xv.79
2360	*Troilus & Cressida*, III.ii.210–11
2508 ff.	*Richard III*, I.iv.9 ff.
2647–51	*Lear*, IV.iv.1–6; IV.iii.17–19
2655	*Troilus & Cressida*, I.ii.71–2, 76–7
2656–60	*Hamlet*, IV.vii.175–83
2667 etc.	*Lear*, III.ii.19–20 etc.
2730	*Tempest*, I.ii.197–8

Perhaps the most teasing detail which could be imagined to link *Tom a Lincoln* with Shakespeare relates to the word *derne*. The author of the play uses it several times (ll. 1842, 2625), in contexts which identify it as belonging to the inflated language of rhetorical passion which is one of his targets. Shakespeare had used the word in *King Lear*, in the scene of the blinding of Gloucester (First Quarto (1608), III.vii.63–4):

> If wolues had at thy gate heard that dearne time
> Thou shouldst haue said, good Porter turne the key,

The First Folio changes the earlier line to read:

> If Wolues had at thy Gate howl'd that sterne time,

If, as recent scholarship maintains, the Folio text represents a revision of the play by Shakespeare after the publication of the Quarto of 1608, and perhaps as late as 1610–11, this particular change could have been motivated by his awareness that *derne* had become a dangerous word to use in a context of serious emotion.

Authorship

After its discovery, the first name attached to the play, however conjecturally, was that of Thomas Heywood. Croft set great store by the presence in the play of an impressive range of Heywood's favourite outlandish vocabularly. His observations were correct, but he did not acknowledge the extent to which even the most idiosyncratic coinages became the common property of Jacobean writers, nor did he allow for the tendency for idiosyncracy so apparent to offer itself as material for parody or imitation.

Tom a Lincoln also displays other characteristics familiar from some of Heywood's plays, although by no means exclusive to them. The mixture of heroic and erotic romance matter with low comedy and clowning had a long history, extending back at least to the 1570s, if not to the first half of the sixteenth century. From the mid-1590s onwards, Heywood was a notable writer in this vein. Like the author of *Tom a Lincoln*, Heywood, in his romantic plays, prefers plot complication and narrative variety to any sustained analytic treatment of character or theme; he likes comic set-pieces and freely uses other characters as mere foils for his clowns; he is intensely patriotic; he uses songs freely and frequently; he has a penchant for creating grieving fathers, and for mad scenes and other climaxes of extravagant rhetorical passion; and the matter of his clowns' speeches is largely made up of food, drink, sex and, on occasion, tobacco. A resourceful parodist would have found plenty to work on here, were it not that some features of Heywood's plays, notably their scenes of verbally inflated passion, already have almost the quality of self-parody. In drama of this kind, the line between what is straight and what is parody is often hard to draw.

Beyond this general congruity, the case for Heywood's authorship rests on three types of evidence: (1) the resemblance of a particular scene in *Tom a Lincoln* to scenes in Heywood's plays, (2) the use of unusual vocabulary of the kind found in Heywood and (3) connections between Heywood and Gray's Inn.

As to the first, Croft rightly indicated that a notable scene in *Tom a Lincoln* directly imitates a scene in Heywood's *The Rape of Lucrece* (printed 1608). He did not observe that two further plays of his contain scenes which also bear a resemblance to it. The scenes in *The Brazen Age* (1613) in which Venus attempts the seduction of Adonis contain merely some parallels of word and action, but the scene of Psyche's spying on the sleeping Cupid in his late play *Love's Mistress* (1636), repeats and adapts the same pattern of action. The three similar scenes are all bedroom scenes. Each starts with an apostrophe to night and proceeds to the discovery and awakening of the sleeper. The paradigm is clearly the rape of Lucrece described in Shakespeare's poem, perhaps reinforced, in its theatrical dimension, by the opening of the final scene of *Othello*.

This is the passage in Heywood's *Rape of Lucrece* (1608 ed., G1):

> *Enter Sextus with his sword drawne and a Taper light.*
>
> *Sex.* Night be as secret as thou art close, as close
> as thou art black and darke, thou ominous Queene
> Of Tenebrouse silence, make this fatall hower,
> as true to Rape as thou hast made it kinde
> To murder and harshe mischiefe: Cinthea maske thy cheeke,
> And all you sparkling Elamentall fires,

Choke vp your beauties in prodigious fogges,
Or be extinct in some thick vaparous clowde,
Least you beholde my practise: I am bound
Vpon a blacke aduenture, on a deede
That must wound vertue, and make beautie bleede. . . .

Lucr. discouerd in her bed

Whoever wrote *Tom a Lincoln*, it is at least clear that its author intended to imitate or parody this scene of Heywood's. Where the scene in *The Rape of Lucrece* ends with Sextus bearing Lucrece off (and that in *Love's Mistress* with Cupid's punishing Psyche's curiosity by disappearing from her), the scene in *Tom a Lincoln* shifts suddenly from the intitial bashful outrage of the hero to a quite different conclusion (1647–57):

Cæ: I ame vnready yet most ready to: shee leps into ye bed:
Red: fye: we haue spoke to much let something doe
Cæ: I ame vndone, yet nothing haue we done
Red: I trust we shall by rising of the sunne
Cæ: knights tongues are swift theyr weapons very slowe
Red: you lye to open, gard yor self belowe
Cæ: I little feare yor forces:
Red: wth my dart
Ile pearce yor target framed [wth] by finest art
Cæ: but drawe the curtaines: for should [here] those heere see
our simple skill ashamed we should bee

The explicitness of this sexual dialogue has many analogues in Heywood, conveniently anthologized in *The Escapes of Jupiter*, in which he turned the erotic episodes of his *Golden Age* and *Silver Age* into a self-contained action. But no known play of Heywood's quite matches what follows. The discreet withdrawal of the lovers leaves the stage clear for Rusticano, whose own version of the events of the night (1659–80) outdoes in sexual frankness anything in Heywood, or indeed in the printed drama of the period in general.

The outlandish Latinate vocabulary in *Tom a Lincoln* certainly calls Heywood to mind. The presence of *infract*, *infortunity*, *delirements* or *trisulked* (perhaps in error for *trisulk*) might indicate his authorship, but it could as well stem from imitation or parody. The contexts in which such words occur often suggest a deliberate intention to write bathetic rant, recalling (say) the multiplicity of unfelt horrors in Heywood's handling of the fall of Troy at the end of *2 The Iron Age*. Equally, the play contains a number of odd words which seem not to bc parallelled in Heywood. Two of these occur together (2068–71):

whoe
came to the queene of fayries wth thee, Ru: whoe was
drunke there for company with thee, Ru: whoe mischieft &
metagrabolizde fower ladyes Collosodiums in one night: Ru: . . .

Metagrabolizde and *Collosodiums* are odd words indeed. OED traces the former to Rabelais, citing Urquhart's translation for its first example.[23] 'Grabolize' is evidently cognate with 'garble'. One clue to 'collosodium' is in another romantic play, *Guy of Warwick*. The clown, Philip Sparrow, having been pinched on the buttock by fairies, exclaims 'do you call these Fairies, a vengeance on them, they have tickled my Collefodiums ifaith'.[24] *Collosodium* and *collefodium* are alike unknown to *OED*, but presumably they are the same word, mildly confused by either Hand C or, more likely, the compositor of *Guy of Warwick*. In favour of *collosodium*, it could be argued that a 'colossal' *sedium* or *sodium* is a self-explanatory synonym for an ample buttock.

In addition to comic words and Latin inkhornisms, the play uses a few words which appear to represent the vocabulary of Rusticano's Lincolnshire. Among these are *phraises* and *kadumbeld* (ll. 788, 1504). Contexts define the former as dishes of eggs and butter made in Lincolnshire, and the latter as a jocular synonym for tipsy. *Froyse*, used by John Taylor in a catalogue of food in *The Great Eater of Kent* (1630, C1), gives a more common spelling of *phraise*, while Rusticano's confusion of the word with 'phrase' may recall both Bardolph's puzzlement about 'word' and 'phrase', and Sir Hugh Evans' fusion of 'words' and 'worts' (*2 Henry IV*, III.ii.69–77; *Merry Wives of Windsor*, I.i.120–1).[25] The case of *kadumbeld* is different: many possibilities are raised by a wide range of apt senses of the root 'cad-' in combination with either 'dumb' or 'humble'.

Heywood's connection with Gray's Inn can be traced to the dedications of three of his plays, *1 Fair Maid of the West*, *2 Fair Maid of the West* (1631), and *1 The Iron Age*, (1632). The first was dedicated to John Othowe (or Athow), who entered the Inn on 16 February 1608, and the others to Thomas Hammond, who was admitted on 29 October 1611.[26] Both men remained there

[23] 'Consider, *Domine*, I have been these eighteen dayes in *metagrabolising* this brave speech' (*The First Book of the Works of Mr Francis Rabelais*, trans. T. Urquhart (1653), Book I, Chapter 19, p. 83). The French original is as follows: 'Auisez, *Domine*, il y a dix-huict iours que ie suis a metagrabouliser ceste belle harangue,' *Les Oeuvres de M. Francois Rabelais* (Lyon, 1599) p. 56. A marginal gloss in the British Library copy (given by Ben Jonson to Thomas Skinner in 1628 and marked with Jonson's own extensive marginalia) reads *excogitare*.

[24] Quoted from the 1661 edition, C1. The play was evidently of a much earlier date.

[25] *Phraise* is listed in *OED* under *froise*, *fraise*, and defined as a 'kind of pancake or omlette, often containing slices of bacon'.

[26] See Foster, *Register*, pp. 116 and 139.

throughout their careers. The link between two members of the Inn who were interested in plays (of the same generation as Morgan Evans), and one putative author of *Tom a Lincoln*, may be—indeed probably is—coincidental. Nothing in the detail of the play suggests an allusion to either Athow or Hammond. Only if examples of their hands have survived at Gray's Inn or elsewhere, may it be possible to test whether either of them was one of the scribes who copied the play. What is certain is Heywood's longstanding friendship with both men, a fact which can only strengthen any hypothesis requiring his involvement in dramatic activity at Gray's Inn.

In total, Croft's attribution of the play to Heywood remains plausible, and is enhanced by several of the points made here. Heywood elsewhere drew on the writings of Richard Johnson for source material, certainly for one play, perhaps for two. Some of his plays bear a range of general and specific resemblances to *Tom a Lincoln*, among them the use of a chorus and dumbshows in the five *Ages* and elsewhere. The Lincolnshire allusions are hardly of a kind or emphatic enough to sustain Professor Bradbrook's conjecture that the play was Gray's Inn satire against Lincoln's Inn. Indeed they are quite compatible with Croft's view that a Lincolnshire author might be involved (although the play does also refer to Oxfordshire and to south Yorkshire). Among the least expected local passages is an extended and affectionate comic 'character' of a country parson, 'our sir Iohn a Lincolne': this is occasioned by no more than Rusticano's mistaking of the name Prester John as 'priest Sir Iohn' (ll. 1924 etc.). Thomas Heywood was the son of a Lincolnshire priest.[27]

Obstacles to the attribution are principally three: the apparently parodic nature of much of *Tom a Lincoln* (although there is no reason why a man may not choose to parody himself); the clumsy and repetitive quality of much of the verse, which is not up to the normal standards of Heywood's known plays, and which contrasts markedly with the achievement of the comic prose; and the implication of the *explicit* that Morgan Evans was more than merely a transcriber.

The quality of the writing need not be too much of a problem. Heywood was both fluent and prolific. His notorious reference to 'two hundred and twenty' plays 'in which I haue had either an entire hand, or at the least a maine finger' (*The English Traveller* (1633), A3) implies that he wrote five or six plays a year over a forty-year career, which also included writing voluminous non-dramatic works. For this reason alone, it may be that some of his plays received less polish than others. The poorish quality of the writing in *Tom a Lincoln* might be easier to reconcile with his more polished performances if one could

[27] A. M. Clark, *Thomas Heywood: Playwright and Miscellanist* (Oxford, 1931), p. 3, records that Robert Heywood was rector of Ashby-cum-Fenby from 15 November 1564 and of Rothwell from 10 June 1575.

believe Francis Kirkman's derogatory explanation of why Heywood's prodigious output was mean and loosely composed.[28]

The problem of Morgan Evans is more difficult to put aside. Professor Bradbrook rightly insisted that Croft's argument for Heywood's authorship faced one major obstacle. The transcript of the play ends, in what may be taken as Morgan's hand, with a Latin *explicit* or colophon:

finis Deo soli gloria
Quam p*er*fecta manent, strenuo p*er*fecta labore
Metra quid exornat? lima, litura, labor

As Bradbrook remarks, the 'couplet contains one false quantity (strĕnuo, which should be strēnuo) and makes an obvious allusion to Horace, *Ars Poetica* 290–294. It may be translated, if *quam* is read as *quae*, 'What adorns the measures that have been completed, made perfect by strenuous toil? Polishing, erasure (the 'blot'), more toil.''[29] The lines alluded to come in a passage in which Horace praises Latin poets for leaving the example of the Greeks to 'sing of deeds at home, whether they have put native tragedies or native comedies upon the stage'. Horace then qualifies the praise with this complaint against the laziness of poets:

si non offenderet unum
quemque poetarum limae labor et mora. vos, o
Pompilius sanguis, carmen reprehendite quod non
multa dies et multa litura coercuit atque
praesectum deciens non castigavit ad unguem.[30]

The commendation of poetic labour in the *explicit* seems out of place at the end of a text remarkable for the lack of polish in its own verse. It is tempting to read the couplet—false quantity and all—as the naïve self-congratulation of an amateur who has done remarkably well in many ways, if hardly to the standard set by Horace. Although the clear error, *quam* for *quae* with which the

[28] According to Kirkman, Heywood 'not only Acted almost every day, but also obliged himself to write a sheet every day, for several years together; but many of his Playes being composed and written loosely in Taverns, occasions them to be so mean.' (Catalogue of English printed plays appended to Corneille's *Nicomede* (1671), 'Advertisement to the Reader', quoted in W. W. Greg, *A Bibliography of the English Printed Drama to the Restoration*, 4 vols. (London, 1939–58), iii. 1353.

[29] Bradbrook, 'A New Jacobean Play', p. 4.

[30] *Ars Poetica*, ll. 290–4. Loeb translation: '[Latin poetry would be supreme] were it not that her poets, one and all, cannot brook the toil and tedium of the file. Do you, O sons of Pompilius, condemn a poem which many a day and many a blot has not restrained and refined ten times over to the test of the close-cut nail.' *Horace: Satires, Epistles and Ars Poetica*, ed. and tr. H. R. Fairclough (Cambridge, Mass., and London, 1929), pp. 474–5.

couplet begins, is easily explained as an error of transcription, it seems unlikely that the lines were written by a professional poet, and merely copied by Evans.

It has been suggested above that the tone of *Tom a Lincoln*, and its treatment of sources, point to some degree of intentional parody. Whether this parodic quality is more compatible with authorship by a professional exponent of the genre parodied, or by a witty and talented amateur (a student or students), can hardly be determined without fuller analysis of the text. There are grounds for supporting each of these views. What is certain is that the play's handling of popular dramatic forms reveals an awareness of the intrinsic absurdity of some features of those forms. Although it lacks the sophistication of (say) Beaumont's *The Knight of the Burning Pestle*, *Tom a Lincoln* is founded on a wide knowledge of the dramatic repertoire of the early years of the seventeenth century, and derives much of its energy from the appreciative impartiality with which it smiles alike at Heywood, Shakespeare and presumably other dramatists, harder to identify today (not to mention poets such as Spenser).

Other Items in the Manuscript

The text of *Tom a Lincoln* ends on Fol. 46b. The remainder of the manuscript (that is, to Fol. 64b) was used as a notebook, and contains eleven other pieces principally six sets of memoranda, three sets of English and two sets of Welsh verses (see above p. xii).

The Memoranda

The hand on Fols. 48–9 and 61b is probably a version of Hand A in the text of the play, that is, of Morgan Evans himself (see Plate 11). It is rushed and scribbled on Fols. 48–9, and the notes may well have been taken from dictation: numbering of items is abandoned after Fol. 48a, and there does not appear to be an order of priorities. Parallels for the spellings 'wief' and 'gieve' can be found in Hand A's pages of the play. The 'sessions' referred to at l. 27 'must be the Great Sessions, a uniquely Welsh court, abolished in the 1830s' whose 'surviving records, both criminal and equity, are deposited in the National Library of Wales' (quotations from Dr Lloyd-Morgan, private communication: see above, note 4, where there are further details about the personal and place names in these memoranda).

The note on Fol. 61b, dated 8 September 1619, is associated with these notes by the repetition of the name Jenkin Lloyd ('my vncle', l. 105), this time as witness to the renewal of a tenancy. The writer of the memorandum identifies himself as the brother of 'Hary Evans': presumably he is, once more, Morgan Evans. His participation in the transaction, together with his uncle and his brother, may imply that his father has died by this date.

The hand of the fragmentary entries on Fols. 50a–51a could again be Hand

A. The dates in the unfinished translations of Merlin's prophecies and destinies, 1616 and 1619, provide a *terminus ad quem* for the earlier contents of the manuscript.

The list of books and other items on Fol. 63b is Hand A's final entry in the manuscript (see Plate 12). The alteration in l. 1 of 'leave' to 'left' implies the physical removal of the manuscript from 'my study', presumably at Gray's Inn, to Evans' 'home' in Wales. The manuscript's presence in Wales from the date of his return home (? 1611–16) to at least 1619 is indicated by the entries following the text of the play. The books listed suggest the reading of a young law student with a literary bent, whose tastes ranged from Cicero or Mantuan to Ovid, Terence and jestbooks (tastes congruous with what one finds in *Tom a Lincoln*). For 'Sir Walwine' in l. 3, see above, p. xi.

English Verses

The fragments of English verse on Fols. 51b and 58b differ in character and quality, although both were probably written by amateurs. The lines on Fol. 51b, which may again (although much less confidently) be assigned to Hand A, were written out in course of composition: the revisions include the marking of almost half of them for deletion (see Plate 13). They express an engagingly naïve response to the first experience of 'a lovinge passion' directed outside the writer's immediate family. The adolescent quality of the sentiments would make this an unlikely exercise for Morgan Evans, who was a grown man by the second decade of the seventeenth century.

The sentiments of the four couplets transcribed on Fol. 58b (perhaps in Hand A) are still adolescent, but rather more cynical. The implied relations between the writer and the whore, mistress and chambermaid alluded to are obscure, even murky: the pervading spirit is one of male sexual self-aggrandisement and erotic fantasy. The tone is not unlike that of several passages in *Tom a Lincoln*.

The most interesting verses are on Fols. 60a–61a. The ballad against female infidelity is clumsy in its syntax, diction, rhythm, rhyme and orthography. The italic hand, not found elsewhere in the manuscript (see Plate 14), is painstaking and insecure, indicating perhaps that the author and scribe are one, although the *explicit* appears to differentiate the anti-Catholic gentleman scribe from the imprisoned author, John Band (who may merit further search in the judicial archives of Herefordshire). Once again the local reference reflects the origins of the manuscript in the Welsh border region.

Welsh Verses

Fols. 62b and 63a are occupied by two short poems in Welsh, written in an unidentified hand (see Plate 15). The first (Fol. 62b, ll. 1–28) is written from the standpoint of a man, complaining of the coolness towards him of the girl he loves or desires, while the second (Fol. 63a, ll. 1–20) is the lament of a man whose close friend or relative has gone across the sea, compounded by the speaker's own enforced absence from his parents and home area. Treatment of themes is fairly conventional. Both are written in a very common metre, with four stresses in the line, one of the free metres associated with poets of lower status than the bards or court poets. The poems may have been intended as songs, or even composed on the pattern of a well-known tune.

Linguistic details indicating origins in eastern or north-eastern Wales include the use of *-e*, not *-a*(*u*), for plurals, and *eisie* (l. 26) for *eisiau*, and the use of *wvlo* and *grio* for 'to weep' (l. 18), instead of *llefain* or *llefen*, which is the normal southern word. English loanwords, notably *sir* for 'cheer', are more likely to suggest the border counties. The literary achievement is modest (as is the case with the English verses). Some of the revisions (for example, l. 23) appear to have been made in the course of transcription, which would suggest that the author was the scribe. Yet there are errors which do not look at all as though they could have come from the author: notably *rwi* where context demands *wnei* (l. 7); *Cam* for *am* (l. 27), where the apparently erroneous *C* may possibly be explained as a slip of the pen or an opening parenthesis; and what looks like *trogar* for *tro ar* (Fol. 63a l. 20), although the *g* may be a blotted deletion.

What follows are literal versions of the two poems (prepared by Professor Ford and revised by Dr Lloyd-Morgan).

(1) Poem on Fol. 62b:

Sad and vexing is all music, every measure displeasing,
And strings and pipes I hear with no great pleasure,
I no longer know the difference between the voice of a pretty cittern,
Or harp, and the mocking cry of owl by night.

Away with happiness, go song, away from me;
Come sadness with your tranquillity, you are welcome;
Now I shall exchange you for mockery;
No longer shall I spend my time so vainly.

Youth is probably not considered sad;
Young men are wont to be glad by night and by day;
Though I am young, I am not happy;
The sombre metre is my proper fee.

What then, dear friend, you appear as a horse
Which chews the bit with his teeth whatever is done;
You, young maiden, or your mistress, are surly to me.
That is the only thing I know which might make you sad.

I am not so foolish, and I'm not boasting,
As to weep or cry or sigh so sad

For the sake of a lovely maid, though so fair her walking,
'Tis not the sour eye of a maid that'll make me lose my mind.

I'm not the man, despite her yellow locks,
Who cannot eat sweet figs from the shop,
Or sleep in a bed [alas, how foolish his mind] because of a fair maid,
But only sigh and stare straight ahead.

I now know what cause there is, alas,
Wanting to see that I've had my bellyfull made you so miserable
You will see the wrong in that, there is some blame upon you,
Before the month of May comes, with its pleasure and delight.

(2) Poem on Fol. 63a:

Heavy-hearted I am from leaving my dear mother and father,
And sadness shall I have from leaving all my friends and my country.
This is no loss, compared to the loss of my dear one;
When I lost his company some grief came upon me.

Sadness to the time he left the land,
A hundred sadnesses to the star which soured my cheer;
Sadness to the sailors, with their sails and oars,
Who helped him to pass, to row across the sea.

A hundred sadnesses to the wind with its slack, weak breeze
That did not break his sails anywhere before his coming to shore.
In the wake of Irish rabble, and wild foolish nation,
May he who sent him never come back.

Unless he returns among all his friends,
Unless he comes to Wales, phoenix of the world,
No smile, for the sake of a dear one, will be seen on the lips,
Nor happiness in the heart: a faithful friend provides that.

If anyone asks, like a mouse in a chest,
For the sake of a dear, beloved one, who would sing so sadly:
A sad man who collected all his senses together,
And a man who will not be happy until a change of the world comes.

Editorial Conventions

The following conventions are used for this edition. Square brackets enclose deletions, except for those around folio numbers ([Fol. 1a] etc.). and where they are the scribe's own marks for beginning or enclosing stage directions (for example, on Fol. 21a, '[Exit]', l. 1250). Angle brackets enclose material which other causes (paper damage, blotting) have removed or made difficult or impossible to decipher. In such cases, dots indicate illegible characters (thus 〈.〉).

Line numbering for the text of the play is continuous, from Fol. 1a to 46b. The other items (poems and memoranda) have their own line numbers. Each line of text in the play and in the other items—including cancelled lines, headings and (where appropriate) stage directions—is numbered separately. Interlineations have been lowered into the text, and noted in the textual footnotes: carets are not printed, but their presence is recorded. The position of elements of the text such as speech-prefixes, stage directions, headings, and indentations is reproduced as exactly as type permits. Slight misalignments have been ignored. Rules and dashes have been printed in the text. The text is printed continuously; blank lines within the text are ignored, except between the stanzas of some songs.

As with any transcription, several letter shapes require editorial decisions, especially in distinguishing between majuscule and minuscule forms (for example, the forms used for *D* and *d* by Hand C: see above, p. xvi). This is also true for the suspension of letter forms, where the intention to raise a letter is not always certain. Variations in the size of letters—between the five hands, but also within the same hand—have been ignored: superscript letters have been printed the same size as the remainder of the text. The position of punctuation above or below the line has been normalized. Irregularities of word-division are generally ignored.

The abbreviations for *er*/*ar*, *per*/*par*, *pro*, and *us* have been expanded, and shown in the text in italic (thus 'neu*er*', l. 2053: see Plate 1). Other contractions are printed as they appear in the text, together with tildes wherever the scribes have used them. Long *s* has been lowered. Final *s* in Hand A resembles the common abbreviation for *es*/*is* (see above, p. xv). The letter is represented here by *s*. Quotation marks " and ⟪ are both rendered as ".

The pages in the Plates have been reproduced full size.

List of Characters

King ARTHUR
ANGELICA, a Court Lady
ANDROGEO, father of ANGELICA
TIME, the Chorus
ABBESS of Lincoln Convent
DORCAS, an old shepherd, foster-father to TOM
TOM A LINCOLN, the Red Rose Knight
CLITOPHON }
MALDO } shepherds' sons of Lincoln
RUSTICANO, the Clown }
PASTORO, father of CLITOPHON
DORUS, father of RUSTICANO
TITYRUS, father of MALDO
Queen GUINIVERE
Sir GALLOWINE
Sir LANCELOT du Lake
Sir TRISTRAM
French Ambassador
Duke of ANJOU
LEWES, King of France
Duke of GUISE
CAELIA, the Fairy Queen
PRESTER JOHN
BELLAMY, Queen to PRESTER JOHN
ANGLITORA, their daughter
Sir LAMORAK
Sir PALAMEDES

Ladies of the Courts of ARTHUR (1), CAELIA (3) and PRESTER JOHN (2 or more)
Lords of the Courts of ARTHUR (Knights of the Round Table) and PRESTER JOHN (4)
Shepherd
Soldier in outlaw band
4 Messengers
Peers of France
2 Mariners; 2 Sailors
People of the kingdom of PRESTER JOHN

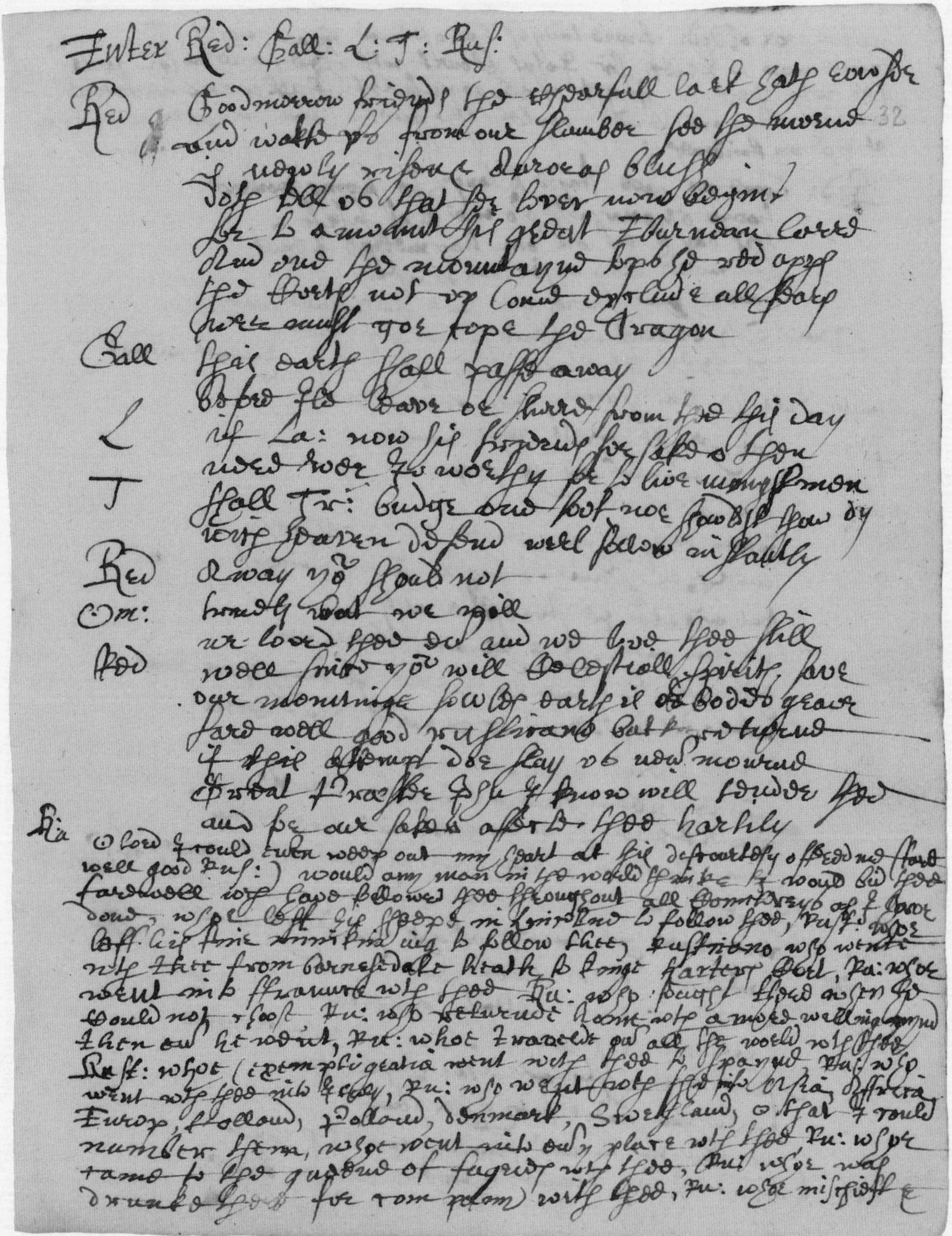

PLATE 1: BRITISH LIBRARY MANUSCRIPT, ADD. 61745, FOL. 32a, *TOM A LINCOLN*, LINES 2032 TO 2070 (HAND A)

Red: Aboord Companions lanch we to the deepe [Exit Red: & his Company]
Heaven thine happy state, blesse, send, & keepe
Kinge Ar: See they are gone come lett vs in to sporte
Fraunce shall knowe, Arthure keeps a princely Courte [Exeunt omnes]

Enter Time

Time Cannot longe be absent, least you stray
and now shall Close the Brittanes by the way
to whome milde Neptune & the powers of sea
the yeare to gether prov'd gently calme
In wch speedy navigation, they see past
Many a monarchs Courte & potentate
Castinge ore Spaine and fruitfull Italy
Europ & Turkey, wth great Affrica
In wch stands auncient Carthage; Barbary
Numedia, Mauritania, wch is ioyned
In Tyngitania, that haue one the west
The Called Ocean, on the north the Straights
of stoute Morocco south Getulia
Caesariensis Mauritania hath
the sea Sardon, leaninge to the North
the mountayn Libia bendinge to the south
yea all the spacious orbe to and the mates
had well nigh coasted, Countreys, kingdomes, states
all, yet all yet now could he heare
the least suspition of his longe sought sire
but left behinde him still a glorious fame
of the round table and of Arthurs name
Nowe at the end of the yeares Navigation
they haue discried a verie famous lande
where how they speede you ere presently shall heare
If yow but lende them an attentiue eare EXIT

Enter Red: Ceal: Lam: Trist: a mariner & Ruffiano

Red Vpon what shore are we arrived speake
what Countrey doe we tread one
Mar: fayry lande,
these say noe man inhabit heare, if soe
nought can wee looke for but death or worse

PLATE 2: FOL. 19b, LINES 1109 TO 1145 (HAND A)

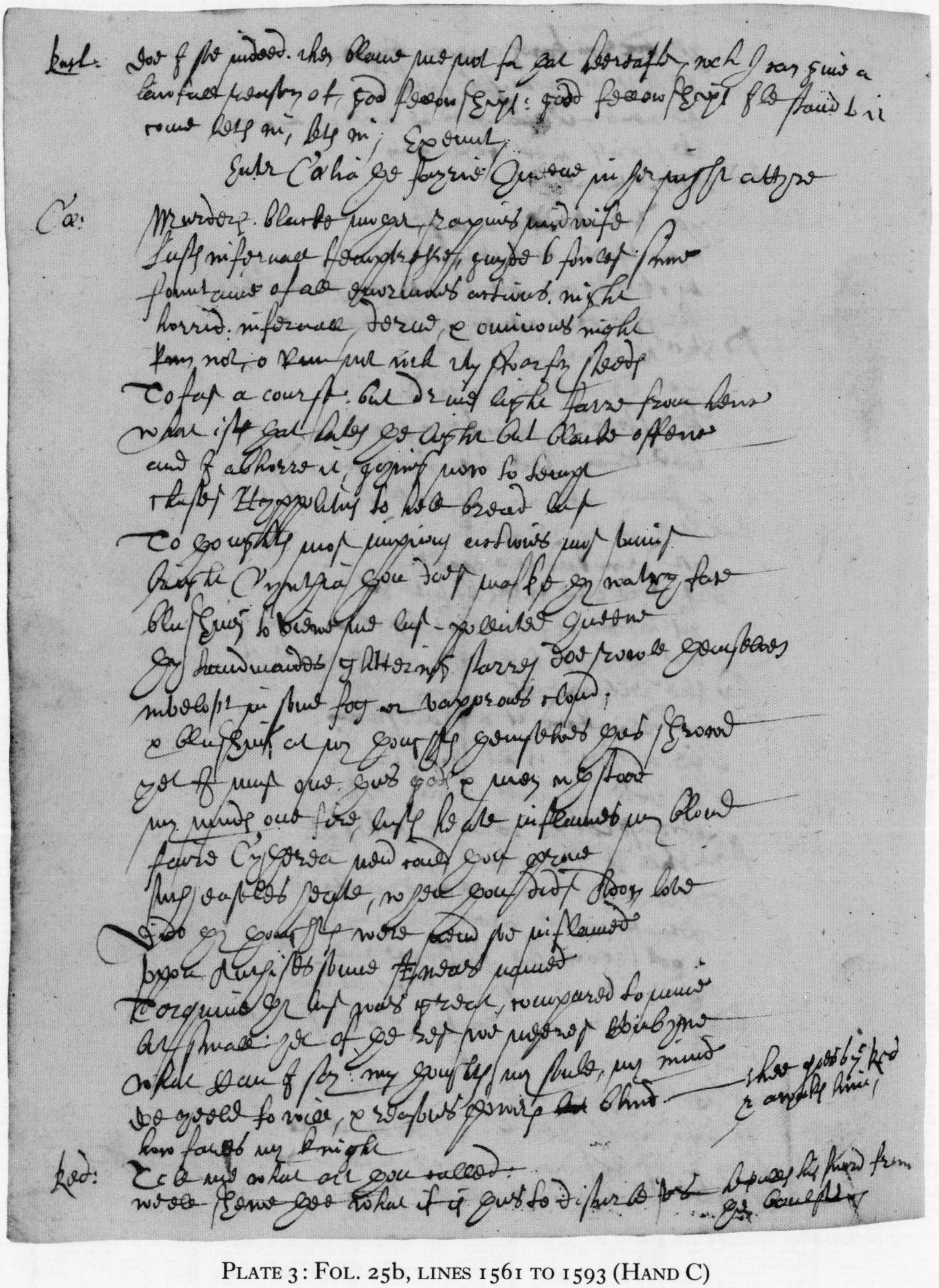

PLATE 3: FOL. 25b, LINES 1561 TO 1593 (HAND C)

meane while sweet princesse comfort to mine age
ioy to my heart and pleasure to my soule
I heare committe unto thy skilfull hand
this mighty knight who by his hardines
hath slaine th' Chymera to our great content
prove Æsculapius ~~[illegible]~~ and recure his wounds.
whose name he caried of th: Redrose knight.

Ang: leave it to mee my lord my skill shall show
~~how~~ how soone the salve his cure, how ist brave knight
why is yor colour chang'd.

Red. Madam I bleed
And gin to faint through too much losse of blood
my wound is deepe and doth require yor arte
its deepe indeed I feele it at my heart — *aside*

Ang: Dread lord wee must entreate yor maiesty
a litle to forbeare the knight's not well.

K. Perhaps his hardy travell this day
by [illegible] him woulde away — (*Exe: K: & and all his court- manet Redrose and Ang:*)

Ang: How fare you sir I'le warrant yor cure soone

Red: Lady my wound is dangerous I feare.
my heart is pierc'd what hope can I expect
unless yor grace alone doe me protect

Ang: Tis out yor mind my lord I'le pawne my word
my selfe will salve it,

Red: you must ioy affoords

Ang: Let's know the depth of it

Red: Oh those [illegible] eies
which [illegible] all earth thy beauty [illegible]
those blazing comets they have made the wounds
and you have pawned yor word to make mee sound
I claime yor promise & you'le keepe yor word,
salve what yor heart and pleasant [illegible] affoord

Ang: ~~[illegible]~~ are you so craftie faith I'le not recall
my vow once made take heart, take hand, take all.
All promise unto thee I [illegible]

Red. I all and more then all I thus resigne — *she kisse him*
~~[illegible]~~ whose [illegible] not my vitall spirits

PLATE 4: FOL. 36a, LINES 2318 TO 2354 (HAND D)

Sheepe hooke farewell and Keepe I bid adieu
for Rusticano cloane forsaketh you
Tom Most harty thankes I yeelde you valiant spirits
bee thou couragious let your mindes be lift
farr farr aboue theis mortall bodies masse
thinke what a chronicle of lastinge prayse
fames tongue the souldiers most affected badge
shall etchd poesy and lowdly make resounde
while were the knighthoods prowesse shalbe crownde
Not farre from hence a vast and open playne

PLATE 5: PORTION OF FOL. 5a, LINES 259 TO 268 (HANDS B AND A)

[illegible] angred, and the [illegible]
in all my life; then I haue now, but I faith tis
to eate & not to fight. Aside
yet be no more then barbarous, [illegible]
and seeing, pitty our calamity.
C. I cannot cast mine eies from off his sight, Aside
they yeeld me such unspeakable delights
braue Christians, you mistake vs, take repose
for euer in our land, as frinds, not foes
be jouiall joyfull frolik what content
these place can yeeld ye take with all [illegible]
Ladies prepare a sumptuous banquet goe Exe. la.

PLATE 6: PORTION OF FOL. 21b, LINES 1282 TO 1293 (HANDS A AND E)

finis Deo soli gloria [Exit]
Quam pfecta manent, strenuo pfecta labore
Metra quid exornat? Lima, litura, labor
Morganus: Evans:

PLATE 7: PORTION OF FOL. 46b, LINES 3091 TO 3095 (HAND A)

Soul: Captaine wee have surprized an aged man
ywrinkled and defatigate with travayls
I come to know yor pleasure to bestowe him

Red: Conduct him hither speedily, be gone [exit Soul:]
Oh tis myne aged father, (Soldier make)
whose tender and paternall care of me
hath forc'd him froward many a weary steppe
onely to seeke me, little he considers
that here his travell shall have period

Mal: When will our parents yor themselves be kinde

Rust: Be kinde saist thou now man now as for my father
would they let ye unhappy halter-sacke goe I warrant yow ye gallowes
will be his end one day & all his, because I would not [illegible]
my cow as hee would have mee, besides hee was spare a great
deale of victualls & was wont to gormundize: to yor [illegible]
[illegible] I never eate above foure morsels of milke or crumbs to a
breakefast in my life [illegible] & [illegible] a morsell of bread & cheese
[illegible] about ye browne loafe & was [illegible]

Eli: Peace, see hee comes, oh tis yor father captaine Enter Dorcas.

Red: father upon my bended knees I crave
yor blessinge and yor pardon

PLATE 8: PORTION OF FOL. 8b, LINES 482 TO 502 (HANDS A AND C)

I can not stand, but doe not I stande as well as the best here
[He falls] so ho when will this rascally tapster come, why boy I say
so ho chamberlaine I am a very rogue but a litle thing would
make me — He falls a sleepe

Qu: Be nowe keept fast, ladies goe, [illegible] some lightes
to guide these knightes unto theyre wished rest
I knowe theyre weary limbes are overtyde
soft beds shall ease them, for good night to all
this night till god with that what ere befall

Red: The like we wish the king and all his trayne — Asyde

Q: nought but thy love can ease my mindes extreame payne — Asyde

Rustican falles in his sleepe. Exeunt omnes

a good fellowe a good fellow in any place in England [illegible] hang up all these base rogues wh[illegible]
will not bee drunke in good companie [illegible]
is this a [illegible] strange dreame [illegible] by my faith my head akes with
hardnes of my lodging [illegible] a vengeance [illegible]
[illegible]
worlds at an end looke how the world [illegible] and tumbles wee are all cast away all cast
away help help help the god god [illegible]
[illegible] of the ship all my friends in Lincolne farewell now now now [illegible]
am I not dead [illegible] I was never in such a pittifull dreame [illegible]

PLATE 9: PORTION OF FOL. 24a, LINES 1463 TO 1483 (HANDS A AND D)

Red: Did never any mortall try his strength
P: Too many worthy knights and all have fell
by this fierce monster that this lowest hell.
Red: which heres a [illegible] for mee by the gods
nay by the brittaine borne
which I esteeme more deare then dearest breath
Ile scape this monster happen life or death
P: Come come you shall not
Red: By thy name great Arthur,
which I esteeme most sacred, by my sword
and by the [illegible] from my [illegible] adore
Ile venge the fiend or never see thee more.
P: Thy resolucons vast.
Red: Thus firme Ile stand
with heart most strong, sword sure, and dauntles hand.
Brit: Had not our captaine spoken first, wee sweare
our lives to hazardize to rid thy feare.
P: what generous spiritts beare brave brittaines [illegible]
heere [illegible] a [illegible] why [illegible]
the spiritts [illegible] a [illegible]
[illegible] life [illegible]
Red: [illegible]
[illegible] of [illegible]
and [illegible] our [illegible]
[illegible] knight.
[illegible] is this fury.
P: Daughter [illegible]
you have not [illegible]
[illegible] on him now.
Red: helpe mee [illegible] Cupid now Aside.
A woman conquers mee [illegible]
Ang: with bashfull modesty a virgins [illegible]
to thee most haughty champion, o forbeare
to cast away thy life to all most deare
yet more then dearest unto [illegible] Aside
earths paragon for magnanimity.

PLATE 10: FOL. 29b, LINES 1855 TO 1890 (HANDS A, D AND C)

Points to be observed by my fathers direction

1 Imprimis where Weeres grounde hath not atturned
tenant unto my father for that [?] whereby
rent is reserved: upon Weeres lease [?]
to pay the chiefe rent of that ground dur-
ing the lease I must enquire of Edward
Edwards whether I shall lose but the rent &
what will become of the [illegible], quere
de for there a fine leuied of the lands by
Richard Edwardes & his wife unto me
whether would [?] if they should

2 If Richard Edwardes will take the
abatement of all reckonings due unto me
& make a generall release or acquittance
which were to release errours made by him
& his wife acknowledged [?] him
the [?] & looke for the old writings
of [illegible] they are at pawne
at Lewis ap [illegible] house of Bishops
Castle

3 There be three exemplifications of a fine
between Richard Edwardes & my father
to be had [?] in [illegible] me
from the [?] be acknowledged
within this 2 or 3 yeares the oldest
then will [illegible] at the last
& then must be [?] for a [illegible]
to be made ready by the clerke
at once & enquire whether there be a barre in
the last fine, & the nature of a barre & how to abate

PLATE 11: FOL. 48a, MEMORANDUM, LINES 1 TO 30

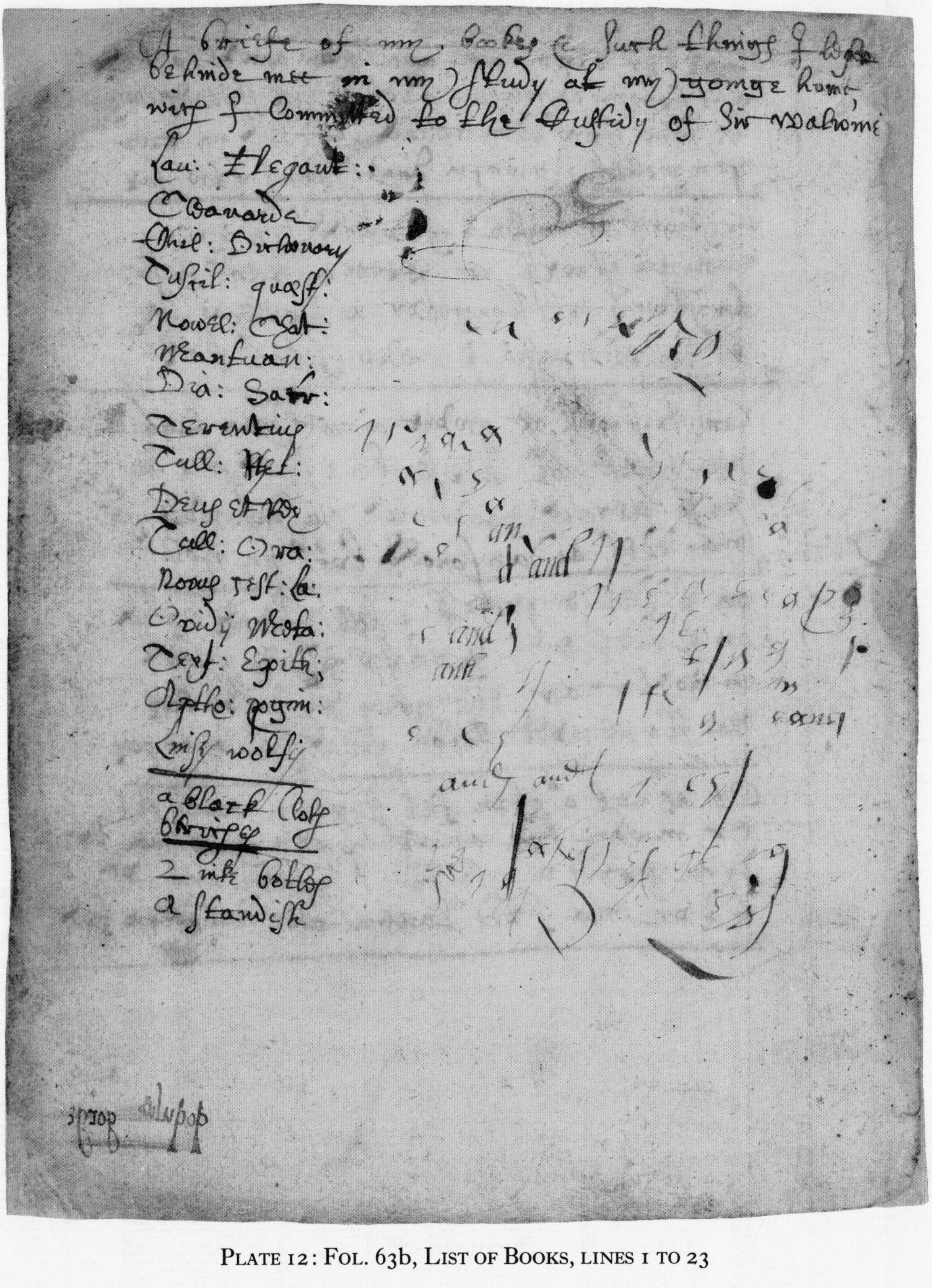

PLATE 12: FOL. 63b, LIST OF BOOKS, LINES 1 TO 23

such is the force of Beuty ioynde with worth
that from all subiects yt can thus bringe foorth
effects of wonder: I that did not knowe
a lovinge passion, onely what I owe
to parents and my frinds, never thought
a constant harte shoulde be by passion wrought
for soone to change that else knowe I see
the sacred power of bewty begetts love
and reared on that rocke yt doth aspire
as high as is the element of fire and I fynde
without all other groundworke not yet the frown
of winde or thunder that can blowe yt downe
that passion beyond nature turnes the mynde
with cherisht in the thought
wheeles of change
yt is a substance of eternity
I that thought not at all
on any love but what was naturall
and brought up with me
but like the flame of burnt wood matter
being by wood supplied doth mount the higher

Plate 13: Fol. 51b, Draft of English Verses, lines 1 to 21

61

The lofty cipruss tre,
That growse so houge and statly
In lickenes is to thee to thee,
Thou hast be trayed mee statly,
For licke the tree that groeth,
And full of frut are barren,
A traytor hast thou bine,
A foule desembling carrion,

Seeke out thy mates else where,
And with desembling woe them,
And as thou hast done mee
Soe doe them and vndoe them
And then thayer songe will be,
The same that I have songe,
That curse ildes the licke of thee,
Thou foule false harted tonge,

This my forsaken songe,
I drawe vnto conclucion,
Though thou hast dune mee wronge,
I wish not thy confucion,
But this I wish to thee,
Of bodi being slender,
That thy next loue may quit my greife,
and may my loue remember,

Writen by a gentelman that cares
as litel for the popes curse as the diuels blesing

Made by John band imprison at herford against
his loue Sibbol hopper

PLATE 14: FOL. 61a, ENGLISH VERSES, LINES 48 TO 75

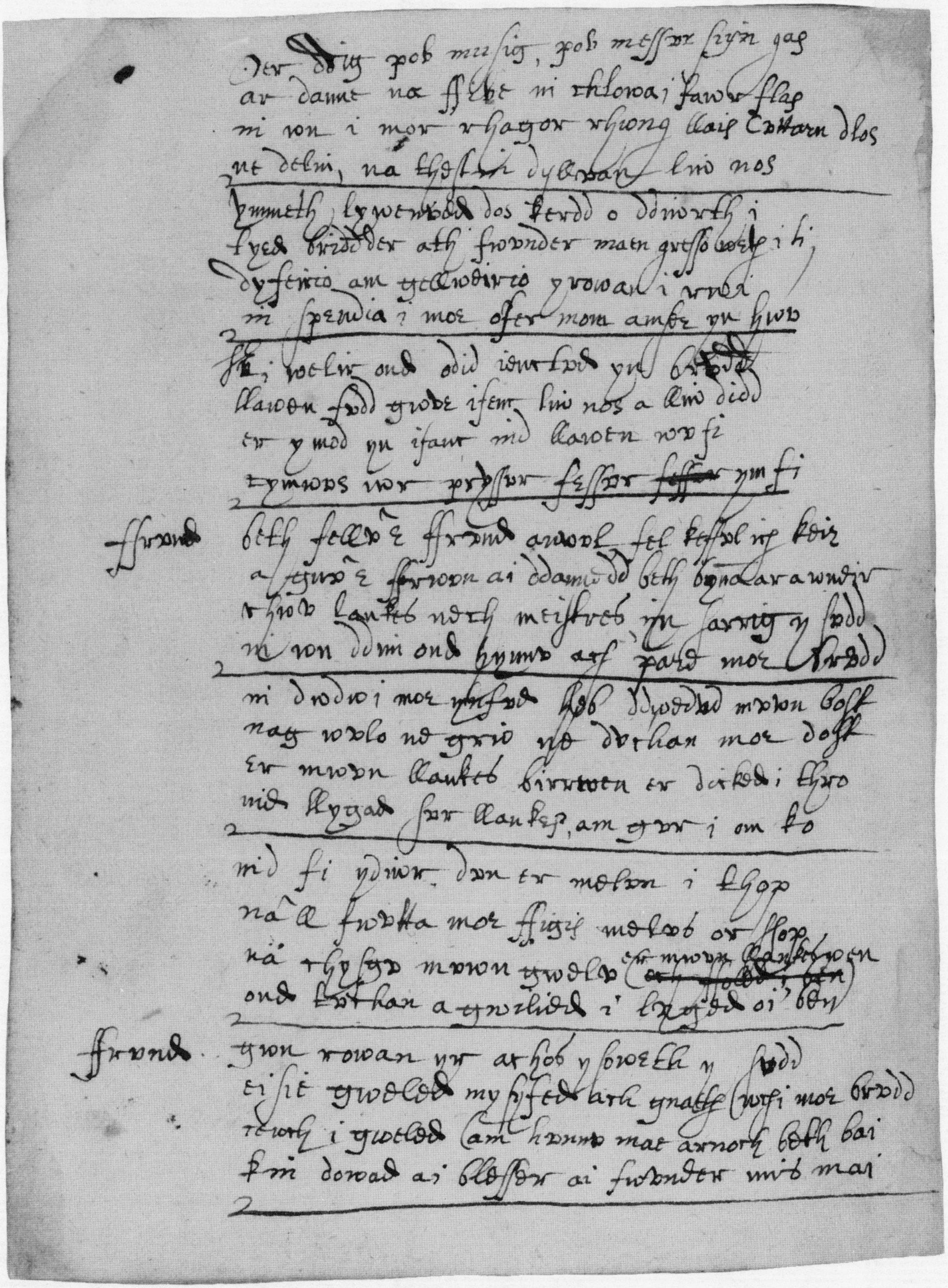

Ter, drig pob messig, pob messwr siyn gas
ar damne na ffebe mi rhlowai fawr flas
mi won i mor rhagor rhiong llais Ewtarn dlos
2 nt delmi, na thestin dyblwan liw nos

kymmeth, lywenbod dos kerdd o ddiwrth i
tyed bridder ath frwnder main gressolwch i hi,
dysfeiro am ycllwdiwro y rowan i wnei
2 mi spendia i mor ofer mom amse yn hwb

ffi, wela ond odid iwnfod yn bwydd
llawen fodd grode ifenc liw nos a llw didd
tr ymod yn ifanc mid llawen wyf fi
2 tymiors iwr pryssur fessyr [struck through: fessyr] ym fi

ffrwnd bth fellwe ffrwnd awol fel kessel ing koir
a tjure ffriwon ai ddamodd bth bynd ar a wndiw
rhiwb lankes nerth meistres yn sarwig y fodd
2 mi won ddim ond hynme arf pard mor Cwrdd

mi drodwi i mor ynfyd hob ddywedd mwlon boff
nag wrlo nd grio no ddrhan mor doff
tr mwyn llankes biwrwen tr dekodi thro
2 mid llygad swr llankes, am gwr i om ko

mid fi ydiwr, dyn tr molwn i khop
na a fwetta mor ffigis melwob or shop
na rhysgd mwyn gwdlw (er mwyn llankes wen) [struck through: illegible]
2 ond fothan a gwrlidd i lygad oi ben

ffrwnd· gwn rowan yn ar hob y sorweth y fodd
ei sit gwdlod mysifed arh gnaths (wifi mor bwydd
rewch i gwdlod (am hwnnw mat arnoch bth bai
2 fri dowad ai blessyr ai fwnder mib mai

Plate 15: Fol. 62b, Welsh Verses, lines 1 to 28

Tom a Lincoln

kinge: Weel live soe privatly non shall see [FOL. 1a]
Ange: excepte the eye of heavens bright maiesty
kinge even what thou wilt doe but com̅aunde & have
Ang: let me live chaste then that is all I crave
sweet lord forbeare to robbe a siely maiden
of that wich lost not all Arabias gowld
can ere recover, kinges are sworne to right
not wronge theyre subiects, knights ought still defend
distressed ladies, not to violate
or offer iniury to any creature
and will y$\bar{o}^{r}$ grace disgrace the name of knighthood
wich till this time y$\bar{o}^{w}$ eu*er* held right deare
In seekinge thus to wronge my chastity
firmely resolûd vnto aeternity
or can y$\bar{o}^{w}$ beinge a kinge, nay demigod
sitt in gods place to gieve the wronged right
ꝑ^{r}ferringe fore falsehood, darkenes light
dare y$\bar{o}^{w}$ I say thus, in his glorious sight
whoe viweth all things, tempte myne honowrs ruin
my father onely seeketh y$\bar{o}^{w}$ to please
yor gracious selfe, o seek not then the fall
of his poore harmelesse daughter: why y$\bar{o}^{r}$ wife
showlde I consente would reave me of my life
not onely that but what I howlde more deare
then life or state, my spotlesse purity
would eu*er* more be branded with this name
kinge Arthures Minion ô a worthy fame
and all the peerlesse deedes wich y$\bar{o}^{w}$ have donne
wilbe eclipsed when y$\bar{o}^{r}$ glasse is runne
king: Angellica vpon my knees I crave
that neu*er* heretofore did stoope to any [she⟨
that I may bwy this ꝑ^{r}ciowse pearle of thee awa⟨
what dost thow hide that fayrest face from me f⟨a]
then shall the world accuse thy hardest heart [FOL. 1b]
and those blest eyes wich will not see me livinge [pulls forth
shall wish to see my liveles body see his knife]
behowld Angellica this fatall knife

FOL. 1 One or more folios missing before the text of the play
1–253 Hand A 5 *robbe*] ^{1}*b* written over *r* *siely*] short dash above *l* 8 *ought*] *t* blotted and uncrossed 10 *iniury*] ^{2}*i* altered from *e* 12 *held*] *l* altered 13 *my*] altered from *ny* 14 *vnto*] first minim of *n* dotted 15 *kinge,*] , low and obscured by *t* in *the* l.16 16 *sitt*] *i* altered, ? from *t* *gieve*] *e* altered from *v* 17 *ꝑ^{r}ferringe*] *i* altered from *e* *fore*] ? for *truth fore* 20 *y$\bar{o}^{w}$*] *y* altered from *h* 22 *wife*] *e* added 25 *purity*] *it* altered from *y* 26 *branded*] *r* altered from *a*

shall instantly bereave me of my life
England adiwe, reporte when I am dead

Angellica thy gretest woe hath bredd,

[he offers to stab himselfe, & she houlds his hands]

Ang: O stay yo[r] hand my liege what do yow meane
will yo[w] believe wee maidens, when at first
wee seeme for to refuse what wee wowld have
werte not for fashions sake, we showld even crave
before men aske, fy fy what were yo[w] dead
to heare a mayde but say she would not wed
king: O fayrest fayre, weare I dead indeed
this would revive me, wherefore heare me speake
thow knowst not distaunt many miles from Lincoln
there is a monastery sumptuous built
thither shalte thow repayre, where weel enioy
Our pleasurable sports without annoy
Ang: but how may I attaine vnto that place
king: p*er*swade thy father that thow wilt embrace
a single life (as vestall virgins vse)
from sigght of worldly ey wich oft entiseth
the purest virgin dost thow see the plott.

[Enter Lady]

La My Gracious soue*ra*igne
The princesse doth expect yo[r] Company [exit Lady]
king: tell her weel p[r]sently attend her p*er*son
farewell Angellica till wee doe meete
and take this token that wee once will greet

[exit kinge]

Ang Thrise farewell to my lord, thus men may see
that kinges rule all with much facility
O fy Angellica recall thy selfe [FOL. 2a]
vnto thy form*er* liberty, darst thow,
soe soone yeld vp thy fort of Chastity
vnto thy vtter downfall⟨,⟩ shall a kinge
at the first siege, have fully in his power
the Cittadell that strongly Can repugne
the greatest force and fury all his force
can lay against yt; noe recall thy mynd
but I have p*ro*misde, yet to violate
an evill vowe is better farre thēn keepe yt

42 *stay*] *t* altered, ? from *h* 51 *built*] *i* inserted 54 *how*] *ho* altered from *y* 64 *will*] *w* written over *g*
66 *Thrise*] *r* altered 73 *repugne*] *g* altered from *n*

well soe yt shalbe, ô but tis a kinge
to whome my word is past he can com̄aund
showld[e] I refuse, nay more can punish me
if that I violat my p*ro*mise made
well then inforcte I yeld, though not inforcte
for tis in me to yeld or not to yeld
Why seinge tis — noe more see wheres my father [enter Androgeo]

And: Angellica yt ioyes my heart introth
and makes me seemingly wax yong agayne
to see thy selfe soe vertuosly disposd
would thow hadst heard what I did ioy to heare
the loving speeches of our gracious queene
how she did prayse thy bashfull modesty
thy well demeanurd affability

Ang: I nere deserv̂d such favour of her grace
Oh why showld I her honowre thus debase [aside]

And: daughter I purpose by the helpe of heaven
to mach yow (if I can soe much prvayle
to that thrise worthy & renowned knight
Sir Launcelott Du Lake, might I live to see [FOL. 2b]
yow thus Conioynd how happy should I bee

Ang: Happy indeed yf happinesse yt be
to live in strife & endlesse emnity
for what is mariag but a marring age
an endles torment eu*er* cloyd wth care
and therefore Ile conclude & firmly howld
(now doupt wth many women on my side)
mariage is wrettched, mariage is a hell
and fewe or non that wed, ere can doe well

Andro: O be not soe invective gentle wench
gainst mariage sacred & most holy rites
for either thou must wed, or ells live chaste
if neither then inconstant lewdly wast

Ang: I graunte yow that (my thrice beloved father
for I secluded from the worlds abuses
men to p*ro*fesse vnspotted purity
vnder yor favowre (most respected sire)

And: How wilt thow bringe ye[t] same to passe (my Guirl)

Ang Not farre from Lincolne, a religiouse howse

83 *or*] *o* altered from *n* 90 *she*] *h* altered, ? from *t* *prayse*] *p* altered from *v* 94 *helpe*] *l* blotted or altered 95 *prvayle*] *v* altered from *r* 99 *Ang :*] *A* altered from *N* 104 *now*] ? for *noe* 106 *fewe*] *fe* amalgamated 107 *Andro :*] *n* inserted 109 *live*] *v*, ? *u* 113 *men*] ? for *mean*

of vestall virgins doth most fittly stand
Cravinge yōr blessinge thither Ile repayre
and be my voyage as my thoughts are fayre

And: Heavens guide my childe, full well I like thy will
if vnder this p̄rtence be hid non ill

Enter tyme as Chorus Exeunt.

I that have bene ere since the world began
I that was[e] since this orbed balls creation
I that have seen huge kingedomes devastācons
Doe heare p̄rsent my selfe to yor still viwve
Ould, aunciant, changinge, eu*er* runninge time
first clad in gowld, next silver, next that brasse
And nowe in Iron, Inferiour to the rest [FOL. 3a]
and yet more heard then all/ & soe ye times are now⟨e⟩
Noe marvayle then/ the times are Irō/ mē scarce demd m̄e
what cannot learnings arte effectuat
time longe since gone, & past yt now calls backe
to tell a story of a princely knight
his birth & fortunes noe lesse strange [and] then rare
wherefore imagine for a twelve months space
kinge Arthure did Angellica embrace
within the Cloyster wth vnlawfull sports
and wanton dalliance, in wich time shee had
kinge Arthures issue, sealed in her wombe
and now behould the p*er*iod of her time
doth app*ro*pinquatt and yt Could not be
but her defaults the Nuns would soone espy
wherefore the kinge with gowlde alures the Abbesse
to be a mid wife to Angellica
wich was effected, & shee salph deliu*er*ed
of a sweet boy, what afterward befell
mark what ensues and yt will plainly tell

A Dumbe shew

Time drawes a curtaine & discou*er*s Angellica in her bed a sleep, the infant lyinge by her, then enters the kinge & the Abbesse whisp*er*ing together the Abbesse takes the childe out of the bed & dep*ar*ts, the kinge alsoe after a litle viwinge of Angellica at an other doore dep*ar*ts, Angell: still sleepinge he being gone drawes the Curtaynes & speaks

122 *Exeunt.*] ? Hand C 123 *world*] *l* altered from *d* 124 *was[e] since*] altered by A from *have seene* in darker ink 125 *kingedomes*] *g* altered from *d* 130–31 A leaves it unclear which phrase should be deleted: *and yet . . . all*, or *& soe . . now ⟨e⟩* 130 *heard*] *e* altered, ? from *o* *all/*] / over , 135 *[and]*] *n* has single minim *then*] interlined above deletion 139 *wanton*] *w* altered 146 *salph*] *p* altered from *l* 147 *what*] originally *who*, *o* altered to *a*, *t* added 155 *drawes*] ? for *Time drawes*

When shee had childed this fayre goodly infant
she fell vnto a sweet and pleasinge sleepe
not once suspectinge what the kinge & Abbesse
intended to the childe whoe greatly fearinge
least her dishonour could not longe be secret
did privatly convay away the boy [FOL. 3b]
leavinge her sleepinge whither twas Convayd
observe the sequel and yow shall p*er*ceave
an Aunciant sheaphard did the babe receave

A Dumbe shew

Enter the Abbesse in hast wth the infant in her arms & kissinge yt
she layes yt downe standing a farre of, enter an ould sheapheard
whoe espyinge the babe takes yt vp greatly reioicinge, & exit, wich
don, the Abbesse wth much ioy dep*ar*teth, then time discou*er*s Angell:
In her bed awake, weepinge & lamentinge, wth the kinge
strivinge to comfort her, wch done time[s] drawes ye curtayne speakinge as before

The Abbesse bare the childe some two miles space
With much celerity vnto a place
the wich is stiled Lincolne, then she layes
this tender infante on a turfe of grasse
adioyninge to an auncients shepheards doore
Whome men calde Dorcas, standinge there vnseen
to see what fortune would betide the babe
when on the suddaine out comes good ould Dorcas
and seeinge (as hee thought) a goodly childe
Lyinge soe neare his howse he takes yt vp
and wth the greatest hast his leggs would beare him
he runns vnto his wife & tells her, Heaven
was nowe p*ro*pitious to there crazy years
in sendinge them a child whoe might releeve
& be a comnfort to them, on whose browe
Time now had gravêd the Caracter of age
Nay wich did ioy them most they fownd the babe
wrapte in a mantle of the purest silke
About whose neck were fownde such prcious iems
as made poore Dorcas farre exceed in wealth
all the Lincolnian pastors, now the Abbesse
seinge the good successe befell her charge
right ioyfully dep*ar*ted, in wich time
Angellica awaked from her slumber

156 *childed*] *l* blotted or altered 159 *childe*] *h* altered 164 *receave*] *v* altered from long *s* 166 [2]*the*] *h* altered 167 *ould*] *ld* amalgamated 172 *two*] *w* altered from *o* 180 *seeinge*] [2]*e* altered from *i* 189 *of*] *f* altered from *r*

and when shee mist her deare & tender infant
Iudge yo^{v} what depth of sorrow shee did feel [Fol. 4a]
but as shee thus lamented came the kinge
and gave a salwe vnto her desp*er*at sowle
makinge her thinke as they to fore consented
that some night trippinge fayry had bereav'd
her infant from her thus in short a time
time breefly hath declard what chaunce befell
this hopefull infant at his happy birth
be yor imaginations kinde spectators
more swifte then thought, run wth me [iudge] thinke the babe
hath fully passed sixteen years of age
the rest he shall p*er*forme vpon the stage
thus with pegasean hast away time flies Ex:
pray lend attentive eare, milde iudginge eyes,

Enter Tom a Lincolne, Clitophon, Maldo, Rusticano with sheephooks

Tom: ye frolick yowths of lincolne here yo^{v} see
our parents sett vs to attend theyre flocks
and basely (like to homebred Clownes) to ly
wth bagge & botle from the morne till night
vpon the downes of Lincolne, whereas wee
are rather borne to wield the branded sword
mauger the force of all that daue gainesay yt
ô let yor myndes be like be like my mounting spirit
wich p*ro*mpts and tells me that I was not borne
to base designm^{ts}, noe, a higher pitch
tis that my Genius ayms at, not like Pan
wth oaten pipe to tune a rowndelay
but wth Bellona sound the drumme & phife
Oh I am ravisht, now me thinks I heare
the armies clangor sowndinge in myne eare
What say yo^{w} lads will yo^{w} (like me) Consente [Fol. 4b]
to leave this life devoyde of all Content

Clito. Brave tom a Lincolne, wch receav'st thy name
from Lincolne where thow first tookst breath
for thee
Ile leave Ile forgett all friends, society

Maldo My mynde concurrs wth Clitophons in this
thine absence Hell, thy p^{r}sence yelds all blisse

199 *salwe*] *lw* altered, ? from *w* *sowle*] *wle* altered and blotted 206 *thinke*] interlined above deletion 209 *pegasean*] *p* has otiose mark of contraction 211 *Lincolne*] *L* altered, ? from *K*; *e* altered 219 *daue*] ? for *dare* 221 *borne*] *o* blotted 222 *pitch*] *c* altered from *h* 225 *Bellona*] *B* altered and blotted 230 *receav'st*] *s* altered or blotted

Rust: As for Rusticano, I will not onely leave my father
Dorus, my mother Sisley, my sister Madge
hange em vp all I care not of a rush for them
but wich is more my prety pigsenie Iugge,
whose goodly p*ar*ts are soe bomination well featurd
especially her secret hidden ones, as to open my
mowth in prayse of them were to carry water
in a rydle, nay they are soe Commonly knowne
to all men of this p*ar*ish (her inward p*ar*ts I mean
as I need not to open the same for in my troth
they are wide inough already Ile make noe
mention of her owtward liniam[ts], for the internallity
of the externallity of any thinge, doth make yt
to be more dearly esteemed but I have lost my
selfe in the p*ro*fundity of her concave privities
And to be short I Rusticano, I defy my father,
I scorne my mother, I detest my sister, &
I vtterly forsake, my fine minikin Iugge wth
whome I haue soe oft vppon wake dayes shake my
heeles at the sum̄er pole, and all to keepe thee swe⟨et⟩
tom, companable societie wherefore thou shalt trau'ell
through this wide worlde takinge my longe farewell in
this poeticall rapture;

Sheepe hooke farewell and sheepe I bid adeiwe [FOL. 5a]
for Rusticano cleane forsaketh you

Tom Most harty thankes I yeelde you valiant spirits
bee then couragious let your minds be lift
farr farr aboue this mortall bodies masse
thinke what a Chronicle of lastinge prayse
fames tongue (the sowldiers most affected badge
shall echo foorth and bowdly make resownde
whiles wee for knightwhoods p*ro*wesse shalbe Crownde
Not farre from hence a vast and open playne
now called barnesdales heath doth fitly stand
where we will live wth magnanimity
and those that passe shall yeld, stay, fight, or dy
Speake are not these Condicōns hownors sonnes

246 *already*] *y* retraced 247 *liniam[ts]*] [1]*i* altered from *e* 248 *externallity*] [2]*t* altered from *y* 251 *Rusticano*] *R* blotted 253 *minikin*] *k* ? altered from *c*

254–64 Hand B 254 *vppon*] *v* altered, ? from *f* or long *s* 257 *farewell*] [2]*l* followed by blot 261 *Tom*] *T* ? altered from *C*

264–318 Hand A: from *of lastinge prayse* 267 *prowesse*] *p* altered from &

Cli: Mal: They are, they are, oh wee will live & dy
ere wee will shrinke a foot in Chivalry
Rust: nay that worde fight and dy can hardly be disgested
Oh how my queasy stomacke, wambles and kisses at yt, fight
or dy quoth a, noe more of that good lad if thow wilt
have Rusticano to be thy boone Companion, If I fight
yt shalbe with a good flitch of bacon, a good peece of
salte powdred beefe, a bowle of Curds and buttermilke
a good Cantell of bread and cheese. let me alone wth
them, if I doe not orecome them all, in an howres
space, then say Rusticano was neu*er* man ofs word ⟨,⟩
but noe fight and dy good Tom, noe fight & dy/
Tam: Then leave vs Rustican⟨o⟩, all we crave
Are stoute Acheevemts and an honored grave
Rust: Not soe Snayles Tom rather then yt showld be sayde [FOL. 5b]
that hardy Rusticano left his fellow Tom after
this fashion, I will soe scufle havinge my fathers
browne bill or wood knife, not onely with Beuis of
Sowthampton that madcap, but the Cock of
my fury beinge once vp, I would let it off with
such a rigorowse rumblinge, ratling Roar⟨in⟩g
Rowlinge noyse, as not all the guies of War⟨w⟩ick
Robin Hoolds, Adam bells, and Clem a the Cloughs
and William a Clowdeslies in the world shalbe
able to wthstand the Ambuscado, or bastinado
wherewith I wowld scarre them: leave thee! ô
impiety, neu*er*, neu*er*, let the glory of my reputacon
be soe mangled with the imputacon of the obliviosity
of good fellowship
Clito, Peace man we heare creat thee gou*er*nowre
of vs and of our forces Tom a Lincolne
and this shalbe the pleadge Confirmes thy right
a lawrell wreath of roses wee will frame
to adorne thy browes from whence accept this name
the Red Rose Knight
Tom Thankes ye Couragious spirits
I take yor p*ro*ffer farre above my meritts

276 *how*] *h* altered from *n* *queasy*] *e* altered or blotted *kisses*] ? for *hisses* 278 *If*] *f* blotted or altered 279 *flitch*] *t* not crossed 280 *salte*] *a* altered from *h* 285 *Rustican⟨o⟩*] *o* smudged 288 *Rusticano*] *c* altered, ? from *n* 290 *Beuis*] *B* begun as *b* 293 *Roar⟨in⟩g*] *in* smudged 294 *War⟨w⟩ick*] *w* smudged 295 *Hoolds*] *sic*; *ld* amalgamated 298 *thee!*] *!* altered from *:* 302 Pen mended 305 *lawrell*] *r* altered, ? from long *s* 309 *meritts*] *me* altered from *ne*

Omnes: Come Come away thy temples beinge Crownd
Weel make the hills and dales with echo sownd
Rust Thus Rusticano leaves his sheep nay more
I leave my Iugge and yet noe filthy whore

Enter ould Dorcas, Pastoro, Dorus, & Titerus

Welmett good neighbours, I am Right gladde
wee are mett together soe happily, Ah neighbors
when wee were yonge lads of Lincolne, I Can assure
yow those were miery times, but nowe our good dayes
are past and gone and all sorrowe goe wth them for me, but y [Fol. 6a]
fayth we haue beene knauish wags: (you knowe neighbor⟨s⟩. well
those tymes when twenty good eggs were sould for a peny: wheate
at sixteene pence a strike, rye & barley very Cheape, a good
vat oxe for vowre shillings. & butter at a peny a quart I
say those tymes are past & gone, past & gone,

pastoro, In feking neyghbour you tell the trereth neighbor, but how sped or
sheepe this rotten yeare,

Dorcas My zonne Tom tells me that vowre of my vattest yewes dyed
yesterday of ye Rott: & shall I tell you neighbours. I had rather
by saintan haue lost fowre nobles

pastoro. Mary neighbor Dorcas itch can assure you I can not but conden⟨e⟩
you fort. for all yor sheepe, especially yeawes are very commo=
=dious. & by the mery mas⟨s⟩e lawe nowe I sweare. that my vnhap=
-py waggestring Clytophon fownd noe lesse then twoe of my suking
lambes yesterday in the Awnder, surceast at a clap.

Dor O bamination & would you thinke or repose neighbors that
the sucking lambe my wife brought vppe at hand should soe
formally yeald the Crowe a pudding. I haue knowen my
wife rise full many a frosty night to giue the poore wretch
somewhat nay if a did but once bleat, there was neyther
my daughter Madge nor any of the houshold servants. but
must runne to it, otherwise shee would soe bethmack, & lay about
them wth her distaffe, as I my self haue tooke my heeles to scape
her sullen fury, my daughter neighbors dyd soe howle & wring
her hands when the lambe was dead, as had not my wife wth
great dacity conswaded her, the slender hearted wench
had fell in a zownd:

Tity: Alacke & well away neighbor Dorus it canot [be] chuse, but these

311 *make*] *k* ? altered 316 *happily*] ^{1}*p* altered from long *s*
319–424 Hand C 322 *rye*] *y* blotted 325 *neyghbour*] *g* altered *trereth*] *er* amalgamated; ? for *trewth*
327 *Dorcas*] *ca*, ? *u* *vowre*] *v* altered from *f* 331 *yeawes*] *y* altered, ? from *l* 334 *Awnder*] ? for *undern*
335 *bamination*] ^{1}*a* altered from *o* 336 *sucking*] *c* altered, ? from first stroke of *k* 338 *wretch*] *c* altered, ? from *h*
341 *bethmack*] *m* interlined with caret; ? for *bethwack*

vnluckeles damnityes should boade some ill. & therefore in my simple pinion twere not amisse, to goe to some wise woman to knowe he screcion in this busines.,

past: By the Roode, twere not ye worst way neighbors. & I can send as I goe [Fol. 6b] homewards. being tis in my way to aske mr parsons conciliation — whether the almanacke dyd not nosticate this Rot of sheepe by my kyrsen dame I haue heard my sonne Clytophon talke in the b[o]uoke of kurnicles. of a pestlence Rot but I thinke in my conscience There was never a quarter soe bominable as this.

Dor But methinkes neighbors the welkin waxeth dym, & it growes [somewhat dym] towards night, I maruaile [my] our sonnes returne not home wth theyr flockes

Enter a shepeheard in hast.,

shepeheard: O neighbors, neghbors. we are vndone, we are vndone, all our zonns haue shewed vs a very fayre paeyre of heeles they haue left theyr flocks & lost themselves, & are even cleane Runne out of the country

Dorcas. oh: oh: oh (he sowndes

shepe: Helpe, helpe for the passion of god helpe: goodman dorcas is gone away in a sownd Rubbs face, wrings nose/ stopps breath, [ho] tweakes little finger, Runne for aquavitae, soe, soe, soe how doe ye goffer Dorcas: how doe ye,

(He recouers.)

Dorcas What was the reason Tom to forsake, thy old hopeles. helpeles father, what shall I say, or how shall I excuse thy flight to thy wofull mother: a ha, art gone, art gone, ile pursue thee, ile followe thee, ile get some flaggy wings. & fly like a Tom titty mouse after thee: thou shallt not serue me thus Rustabella, saddle my pye bald mare: ile not eate a bit wench I must haue. will haue, ought to haue, my Tom, my sonne, my Child: I Come boy I come:

(Exit Running)

Dor: Doe ye see this neighbours: would it not grieue & pitty a mans heart to [Fol. 7a] see a man that talkt soe Renable even now. to Run thus besides his witts talking wthout screcon: you may see what twoe much Tidling (in not suffering the wind to blowe on them) will doe but Come lets in & Comfort his heauy heart, come lets goe, lets goe on gods name

Exeunt at one doore: Enter Dor: at another.,

350 *he*] ? for *her* 355 *b[o]uoke*] *u* interlined above deletion with caret; *e* blotted 356 *There*] *T* altered, ? from *b* 362 *paeyre*] *ey* altered from *p* *left*] *l* altered from *f*; *f* altered from *r* 366 *is*] *s* ? altered 377 3*my*] *y* retraced or altered 378 *boy*] *oy* altered from *y* 383 *to*] or *too* *on*] *o* formed as *v*

Dorc: Ha tis true, tis true, a was counted the nimblest youth in all lincolne and when I had bred him vppe wth griefe & sorrowe, he then — forsooke me, why should he be soe wretchedly vngratefull noe more to pitty me his aged father, but see, see, I tooke him vppe at my doore: Nurst him, fosterd him, as [he] if he had beene mine owne & when I had done all that could be done, he casts away himself ah vngratious Impe, ah luckles Dorcas, wretched old man, teare thy siluer hayres, wring thy wythered hands, for he is gone that should be thy comfort, when age doth sum̄on thee to thy graue: can I liue? can I breath? can I stand here & Raue: when Tom a Lincolnes gone? sure, sure, he had some cause of absence, he was ever kind, ever courteous, ever affable, ever mild, ever gentle, had I comaunded, he would obay: did my wife bid goe he would Run & shall I leaue vnsought soe good a sonne, noe, noe, soe long as my feeble legs will beare me, soe long Ile seeke thee out, & [is ist] if I finde thee, thrice happy I: if not vnknowne in some strange place Ile dye. Exit.,

Enter Redrose knight, wth a garland of Red Roses: Clitophon Maldo Rusticano wth Roses in [.h.] theire hats

Red: we nowe are safe arriued [at] at the port
our valours barke, long wisht to anchor at
wherefore/ heroike spiritts/ shewe yor selves
like to the followers of the Red Rose knight
advance our standard, let the Rose be spread
and proue couragious. s:foote (me thinkes I soare./
Beyond the straine of com̄on knighthoods name [Fol. 7b]
Honour I aime at & eternall fame
Me thinke the Heroes of the former tyme
were not of force to Cope or tugge wth me
in single opposition, Ioues sonnes stroakes
could not offend vs: did they quell huge oakes
but to our busines, let not violence,
bee deemed Captaine of our strong array
despoile not any poore men of theyr treasure
" as men doe sowe, soe shall they Reape theyr measure

Rust: Reape quoth'st, you put into my head a pretty Iest I once did, nowe you talke of Reping and thus it was, when I went wth my grand-father on aday in haruest to reapinge there were in the field a reapinge a great many men & woemen, but most wenches

389 *wretchedly*] *c* altered from *h* 393 *wretched*] *c* altered from *h* 398 *gentle, had*] , obscured by *h* 404 *Maldo*] *a* altered, ? from *u* 405 *[.h.]* deleted by smudging, ? *th* 411 *s :foote*] *:* combines ' and . 413 *aime*] *m* has two minims 418 *but*] *b* altered, ? from *m*

424–92 Hand A: from *to reapinge*

yet nere a maide amongst them all (as I thinke there
are fewe or non heare p^{r}sent, nowe yt chaunced y^{t}
I beinge a well sett striplinge, as yo^{w} see cast
my glaringe ey vpon a yonge ronsifull Virago
one of the smuggest lasses there p^{r}sent, & to be shorte
I fell ore shoose in love wth her, and beinge greatly
enambled of her cherry cheekt countenance, I watcht
her narrowly goinge homewards, and quickly ou*er*takinge
of her I went ou*er* her, I would say I orewent her,
in wich goinge ore or oregoinge wich yo^{w} will⟨,⟩ the
bounsinge lasse did soe labour that at length she cleane
orewent mee, and gave such a Coolinge carde to my
Courage that yt droopte and held downe his head like a
tired Iade, and I was soe ashamed that p*ro*pria fœminei
generis not soe worthy as the masculine, showlde after such
a maner quayle the Courage of p*ro*pria quæ marib*us*
Nay shee would have coolde the Courage of the best
rider here, soone vnhorst him, let him have held her to yt
nere soe heard

Cl: six Merchaunts landed with six thowsand Crownes [Fol. 8a]
wee tooke for hansell at o^{r} first arivall

Rus: I, I, we tooke em and orecom em, I was on meark that

Red: what did they gallantly withstand the onsett

Mal: yea truely did they with great fortitude
the batle longe stood douptfull, in the end
wee ou*er*came them, yonder they attend
yor will and pleasure

Red: O vnheard of valowre

Rust: Nay did not I say what I would doe if I were once
angred, why? I am a very rogue but eu*er*y stroke
I strooke, nay eu*er*y time I lifte vp my sword, I strok
three inches deepe in to there flesh

Clit: I Ile be sworne for thee for thow nere soe much as
toutcht yt, Nay when wee fought thou ranst away
as fast as thy leggs Could cary thee

Red: O I could envy at yor matchlesse worths
because I was not p*ar*tener of yor stroaks
my vaynes doe daunce within mee when I heare
yor first attempts devoyde of dastard feare

426 *I*] altered from *t* 432 *of*] *f* altered, ? from *r* 436 *she*] *he* altered 451 *them*,] , far below line
452 *pleasure*] *r* altered 456 *nay*] *y* altered *lifte*] *l* altered 458 *soe*] *e* altered 464 *dastard*] *r* altered, ? from *f*

heareafter Ile be on for wel'te app*er*es
not he deserves that equally not shares
Rus: say yo^{w} soe Captaine, and by the valowre of myne arme
(noe small oath I assure yo^{w}) Ile soe fitt yo^{w} eu*er* heare
after, that if ere I fight and yo^{w} will doe yt for me
I pray god I may neu*er* more eat bagpoodinge or rusty
bacon more hangde vp in the Chimney for three years
to gether, and that I wowld not for all the wealth
much lesse for all the honesty the gripingst vserer
in the land hath rakte and scrapte to gether by bills
and bands, Nou*er*int vniu*er*si p*er* presentes, habeas Corpus,
Capias vt legatū, non affidavits, and such other quircks
and quidities of legerdemayne, by wich these sutle [Fol. 8b]
headed turners, (what ist yo^{w} call em) doe eat more
money in a month, then the most Riotows spendthrift
can cast away, in wine, drabbs, and Tobacko in a
whole twelvemonth Enter Souldier
Soul: Captayne wee have suprized an aged man
vnwieldy and defatigat with travayle
I Come to know yor pleasure to bestowe him.
Red Conducte him hither speedily, begone exit Soul:
Oh tis myne aged father, (fellowe mates)
whose tender and paternall care of me
thath forĉte him forward many a weary steppe
onely to seeke me, litle he Coniectures
that here his travell shall have p*er*iod
Mal: When will o^{r} parents p*r*ove themselves soe kinde
Rust: soe kynde sayst thou neu*er* man neu*er* as for my father
heele say let the vnhappy haltersacke goe, I warrant yo^{u} the gallowes
wilbe his end one day & all this is, because I could neu*er* varme
my oxen as hee would haue mee, besides hee will spare a great
deale of victualls I was wont to gormundize: & yet Ile ⟨be⟩
sworne. I never eate aboue foure messes of milke or cruds to a
breakefast in my life vnles I tooke a morsell of bread & Cheese
Round about the browne loafe & was that soe much trow y^{e}.,
Cli: Peace, see hee comes, oh tis yor father captaine (Enter Dorcas.)
Red: father vpon my bended knee I craue
yor blessinge and yor pardon
Dorc: Ryse, sonne: Ryse

470 *bagpoodinge*] *p* altered, ? from long *s* 476 *vt*] *v* resembles *o* 477 *sutle*] *e* altered and blotted 486 *mates*] blot above *m*
492–573 Hand C: from *as for my father* 496 ⟨*be*⟩] smudged 497 *messes*] ²*s* formed as *r*

And wipe these teares from of thy fathers eyes
whoe ioyes to see thee, (not to see thee heere
what caused thee thus my deare & tender boy
to leaue thy parents ou*er*cloyed wth care
thy mother sits wringing her aged hands
and sayes: sweet Tom a Lincolne tell me why
Thou hast forsaken me, when / god knowes/ I [FOL. 9a]
haue wearyed mine age-benummed-lymbs
in hope to find thee wch hast lost thy life

Rust: Chide him on gods name, gotter Dorcas, for if he had not beene, I had nowe beene keeping my fathers sheepe in Lincolne parishe, and how doe all our friends there, well: How does spruse Dicke, fine Harry lofty Tom, longe George, lecherous franke, Capring Tayler, sober will. stronge Peeter, nimble Roger, in a word: how doe all those mad Rascales y fayth they are the brauest boyes, that ever danced after a taber and pipe.,

Red: Age honour'd father heauen knowes my heart
how I doe honour & Respect you (both/
nor was it (as you deeme/ ingratitude
that made me leaue you, but a loue to armes
and first shall phœbus leaue the colour'd sky
ere I renounce honour or Chiualry

Dor: Returne deare sonne? Returne wth teare-wet-eyes
thine aged father craues it at thy hands
thou shallt noe more attend the milke white flockes
nor [the] lye vpon the downes wth bag & pipe[s]
doe what thou wilt & promise to Returne
if not this breast shall neu*er* Ioy but mourne

Red: vpon my bended knees see I entreate you
to Cease yor earnest suite (most carefull syre
oh let me still obtaine what I desyre.

Dor: Carefull doest Call me, full of cares indeed
my brest, my mind, my soule, my hart doth bleed.

Red: My Resolution is irrevocable

Dor: O tis dishonorable gentle boy
to spend thy tyme in spoiles & Robbery
depriuing men of that wch they obtaine
wth toyling labour, & heart piercing paine

[Red: I ame irrevocable: Dor:]

Red: I ame inexorable./ [FOL. 9b]

506 *tender*] *nd* imperfectly formed and unclear 513 *gotter*] *e* resembles *o*; ? for *goffer* 526 2*Returne*] *n* altered, ? from *e* 528 *milke*] *ke* amalgamated 529 *pipe[s]*] *s* smudged out

Dor: Ist eene soe.
Canot these teares or sights ought mollify
thine adamantyne breast? wch would make mild
the fiercest Tigres of Hircania
and make them pitty me? is all my care
wch I haue vainely spent to foster thee
now turned to this? oh I foole that I am
“ the whelpe is ever like vnto ye damme
“ that whelpt it first, & soe art thou, for know
(o thou degenerate from natures kind)
thou art noe child of mine but (as I thinke/
whelpe to some Tigresse, or some Lyonesse
I found thee at my doore layd on the ground
a pray for fowles, yet see I tooke thee vppe
and wth great care haue nourisht thee to this
thus to contemne [thee] mee oh this breakes my heart
Heauens take my soule, liue wretched as thou art. Moritur

Red: Helpe, helpe for gods sake helpe my followers
Reuiue him if it be possible, not stirre?
oh me most wretched and infortunate
whence is it that I haue deserud these woes
ye gratious heavens, let a poore youth aske
wherein he hath soe farre transgresst yor lawes
that you should heape a moles of such terrours
vpon mine (as yet) vnexperienct yeares
first that vnhappy I should be the death
of him that causeles hath preserued my life
next that I should be soe involud wih crosses
as not to knowe my byrth nor parentage
whether legittimate or basely borne
what shall I say would any prsent see [Fol. 10a]
blacke griefs Idæa, cast yor eyes on me

Cl: brave captayne be not soe æffeminat
stoope not to fæmal passion, this I fynde
if sorrowes great, farre greaters valowrs mynde
how [have–] will yow have disposde those traffique men

Rust: Com[m]e Come leader hange sorrowe, care will
kill [the] a catt as the sayinge is neu*er* lament man,
for hees gone and wee must goe after him.

545 *sights*] ? for *sighes* 557 *vppe*] ¹*p* altered or blotted 566 *farre*] ¹*r* altered 573 *whether*] *r* altered or touched up 574–742 Hand A 577 *fynde*] *y* altered from *r* 579 *will*] interlined above deletion *disposde*] ¹*d* altered, ? from *h* or *l*; *e* added 581 *kill*] *il* altered, ? from *n* *a*] interlined above deletion

on my troth I would my father weare dead
in his turne to ease thy sorrow, I am sure I showld
loose nothinge by yt for I am his heyre and
all the sonnes he has, well Ile keepe my selfe
out of deaths cluttches, if a play noe fayrer play

Red: Thow liuelesse body of the mildest man
dame nature eu*er* bred, see thus Ile honowre
thy ceremonial rites and Obsequies
three thowsand Crownes I offer to thy love
erectinge for thee a farre richer tombe
then eu*er* Mausols was, three thowsand more
I giue for to compose of p*er*fecte mettall
a massy bell stilde by succeedinge tymes
Great Tom a Lincolne, & the marchants heare
to see our will accomplisht, this weel doe
in memory of him that lov'd vs soe

Exeunt

Sounde: Enter Kinge Arthure, Queen Gwyniu*er*, Gallovine,
Launcelott, Tristram with others

K Sir Gallowine and yow appr*o*ved knights [Fol. 10b]
of Arthures and his famowse Cort
yor foreward sperits eu*er*y ey can witnesse
but in especcially Launcelott and my Nephew
brave Gallowine have won the diadem
that was p*ro*posed, Tristrams manly arme
was a Cop*ar*tn*er* wth yow, oh yow three
are mirrours of the world for chivalry

Gall: yow are to p*ar*tiall, in yor royall censure
my royall vncle oh yt is not glory
that gives my sword edge, here are knights surpasse
I am the weakest, but yet bleedinge scarrs
shall say Ile fight for this in bloud staynd warres

K Nephew wee much aplaude thy modest answer
yet are inforcte sweet vertues prayse to singe
Cleare are the fountaynes, Run from such a springe

L fame honored sou*er*aigne yov give my acts
causelesse above the rest, to high a pitch
Sfoot all I say is this what ere betide
this sword thine vtmost p*er*ill shall abide

584 *showld*] *s* altered from *h* 585 *heyre*] *y* altered from *a* 596 *marchants*] *t* altered or retraced 603 *Arthures*] ? for *Arthures Table* 614 *this*] ? for *thee* *staynd*] *nd* amalgamated 615 *modest*] *o* altered or blotted 617 *springe*] *sp* altered from *ki*: *ri* interlined 618 *soueraigne*] *n* altered from *e*

T knights tongues are blunt, alwayes theyr swords cut keen
My ffawchion is my fluent Orator
he loves me dearest whoe his valowre shewes
by forcinge stroaks, & deepest wounding blowes.
All that I say yor grace I doe intreat
giue p*ro*wesse prayse & eu*er* make yt great
K weel suffragat thy will (right hardy knight)
for fame & honowre whetts a sowldiers sword
Oh yt Corroberats, the warriowrs arme.
Why dare we empty all our vaynes in warrs? [FOL. 11a]
why are we characterd wth wounds and scarrs?
why dare we all things but for honowres name;
and vertues prize o[⟨.⟩] repetations fame
Enter messenger
Mess: Thrise happy & thris worthy Englands kinge
I bringe thee suddayne & vnlookt for newes
there are a route of rebells newly swarmde
at Barnesdales heath wher, as thy robbe & spoyle
All weary Passengers & borderinge townes
K Whose the Cōmaunder of this rascall Crewe
Mess: The Redrose knight they stile him, and by some
stout Tom a Lincolne, but be he what he will
I tell yor ma^{ts}, true Charecters
of bright Nobility are stampte & sealde
ins manlike Countenance, although rakte vp
In servile basenes somewhat led amisse
by yowthfull folly
K Didste thou eu*er* see
or heare what order he observes and keepes
Mess: Oh yes with admiration have I viwede
the well Composed order of his Campe
for with such ma^{ts} he beares him selfe
nay with soe good discretion governs all
as there is none coulde truly deem, but hes
descended from some princely p*ro*geny
yet all the Countrey knowes assuredly
a sheapherd was his father named Dorcas
Of happy Lincolne where he breathed first [FOL. 11b]

624 *loves*] *re* altered to *es* by change of *e* to *s* 625 *wounding*] *u* unclear 628 *suffragat*] *g* altered 634 *o[⟨.⟩]*] interlineation above deleted letter unclear 639 *wher, as*] originally *where* with comma under ^{2}*e*: ^{2}*e* altered to *a* and *s* added *thy*] ? for *they* 641 *Whose*] *W* ? altered, ? from *sh* 642 *Redrose*] *d* altered, ? from *f* 643 *Tom*] *T* altered from *t* 644, 653 *ma^{ts}*] ? for *maiestie* 646 *manlike*] *n* altered from *l* 649 *Didste*] *D* altered from *d* 651 *viwede*] *ed* amalgamated 654 *governs*] *n* has three minims 655 *none*] *e* altered *coulde*] *co* altered from *w* *hes*] *s* altered, ? from *e*

Nay more, yf those that passe by force of armes,
Can conquer any of his Company
He doth dismisse them salphly as they Came
not wrongde in substance, body ⟨,⟩ goods or name
K Weel soone Confront his fury (messenger)
and all his troope (if soe they dare withstande vs,)
rather then our poore subiects be distrest
yet fyrst thy prayses have soe much ꝑ[r]vaylde
weel see yf that fayre means will make him yeld
if not weel force him maugre all his force
to stoope & humbly bend vnto our feet
to good for traytors, and for rebells meet
Brave Tristrā, sir Launcelott & sir Gallowine
Goe arme yo[r] selves and mount yo[r] fiery steeds
and ride to Barnesdale heath, where in our name
Our p*ar*done wth our love to them p*ro*clayme
Condition̂de they in quiet sorte returne
vnto theyre form*er* habitations
onely bringe Tom a Lyncolne salph to Court
whome I desiere to see fors good reporte
Omnes: If he refuse by all our hopes we sweare
weel dragge him hither without dread or feare
making him lowe summissive to thy knee
and iustly pay for his disloyalty
K If he refuse our kingly p*ro*ffer doe soe
Om: wee soe intende, farewell, stout Redrose Knight
Ext: om: Come pleasde, if not wee vowe thow shalte by might
manet k: All tokens howlde in Lincolne was he borne
K fownd at that sheapherds doore the Abbesse left him
That causde ould Dorcas take him for his sonne [FOL. 12a]
And name him Tom a Lincolne, nay whats more
did not the nuncius playnly testify
that shyninge sparkes of high borne parentage
were lively seated in his Comely visowre
O tis thy Sonne all signes, all signes Concurre
to make a resolution of this doubte
light shewe thy selfe to truth and make yt good
that Tome a Lincolnes come of Arthurs blood

Exit

660 *of*] *o* altered from *b* 667 *yet*] *y* altered from *f* *fyrst*] *y* altered from *r* *thy*] *y* altered from *e* 668 *fayre*] *e* altered *will*] w blotted 673 *steeds*] interlined above caret 679 *desiere*] *d* altered, ? from *b* 682 *lowe*] ? for *bowe* *summissive*] [1]*m* altered from *b* 691 *did*] [1]*d* altered from *n* 692 *shyninge*] *y* altered from first of six minims of *inin* 693 *lively*] *v* altered

Enter Rusticano runninge hastily: Alarme

Now fy vpon yt whoe woulde live as we Robin Hoods doe not a munit of⟨t⟩ an hower but heres such slashinge and hewinge as yt grieves my very heart, I forsooke Lincolne mine awne Countrey, to be in daunger of my life eu*er*y while stitch, I sweare we cannot be accused of negligens, or sloth in our vocation, for we are neu*er* idle but takinge of purses, searchinge of packs, fightinge or Ioustinge with one another for euen now at this $\overset{r}{\text{p}}$sent time, iij^{re} Carters I wold say Courtiers, iij knights of kinge Karters Rownd stable, I would say table, these iij knights have defide our Captaine at a mortall defray, and he yelds to goe to them to the kings Court, if either of them Can vnhorse or vanquish him, he had vnhorsed one of them from his horse ere I came away, Nowe Sir I beinge very kinde hearted, could not for pitty see my Captaine vnhorst, as I feare me he wilbe, hearke they be still at yt, they doe soe whote & shoot, but I doe not love such squablinge, I will therefore, very fayrely lay me down⟨e⟩ till they Come, but s⟨.⟩e where they are Comminge, all friends⟨,⟩ I hope

Enter Redrose Knight, Gall: Laun: Tris: Clit: Maldo, [FOL. 12b]

Gall: By all my hopes I can not but admire
(vnlesse im̄ortall Iove hath lente thee strength)
to see such vallour in one armed knight
soe stoutly to resist our greatest might

Laun: I vanquisht Tarquine, at three mighty blowes
Slew that vntamed Gyant Brandevant
vanquisht a hidious dragon, thowsands more
yet neu*er* felt such manlike force before

Trist: The pagan Pallamede, I thrise subdude
and made him turne a Christian, Lamorack
(the terror to his foes) that princely knight
vnhorst I often, and that worthy knight
(that fought against my trecherowes vncle (Marke,)
I wounded wth his owne impoysoned sword
soe that he dide, all this sure have I done
and (but by thee) I nêre was ou*er*come

Red: What mean y$\overset{w}{\text{o}}$ knights, twas fortune, not my force

700 *vpon*] *o* altered 701 *slashinge*] *l* altered from *h* 708 *wold*] *l* altered from *r* 710 *I*] altered, ? from long *s* 717 *whote*] *wh* blotted 719 *friends*⟨,⟩] *s* added over , 721 Pen trimmed 727 *hidious*] *hi* altered from *th* 733 *Marke,*] *M* altered from *m*; *e* added over ,

by wich yo^{w} three, I onely did vnhorse
yo^{w} may Commend my duty to my lorde
Ile eu*er* for him wield this branded sword

Gall: Thow noe lesse Courteows then Coragiows yo^{wth}
the kinge hath p*ar*donde thee & all thy trayne
And prayes thee come along to court with vs.

Lan. This had wee told thee free as now wee stand
had wee beene from thy strokes and Iouelike hand.

Red: you had beleeue mee, ô most gracious prince
is it not enough to pardon my reuolt
but also send thy gallantst knights for mee,
well werȩ the world to oppose thee thou shouldst know
And they should feele, Ide make them humbly bow
wee doe dismisse yo^{u} ancient fellow mates
the heauens will soe and wee yeld to fates.
take all the got and giue the poore
and helping heauen will encrease yor store

Cl: Maldo. well tis noe boote to striue wee bid adieu
weele euer after to our king proue true. exit Cli. and Maldo.

Rusti: you shall not bee soe shift of mee thats flat, for I dare not for both my eares goe home [FOL. 13a] againe for my mother will scould like a butter whore, besides I know my father will soe belambskinne my sides wth a good crabtree cudgell y^{t} I shall neuer enioy faire day after [,] it, therefore either let mee, wherefore either let mee goe wth thee, or [.] in good fayth Ile presently goe hang my selfe

Red: Defend it heauens, are yo^{u} pleased lords for to accept him in yor company
Ile giue my word his mirth will much delight yo^{u}.

Om: with all our hearts a merry freind they say
may well be termed a charret in the way.

Rust: How, a charret o I should make a braue one to carry our ladies of the court but hearke yo^{u} mee how must I and my master carry our selues in the court I pray you shew vs lest wee bee accounted for nouices or (as at the vniuersity) they should take vs for freshmen.

Trist: Shall I instruct thee.

Rus: I for gods sake.

Tris: why then sir if yo^{u} wouldst seeme one of the gallantst courters yo^{u} must court yor lady at the first sight wth a congy

Rust: what doth they loue congers? haue they such desire of fish?

Trist: Oh yo^{u} mistake mee a congy is a kisse or a smacke.

742 &] altered, ? from *o*
743–831 Hand D 749 *well*] *ll* altered, ? from *e* 753 *got*] ? for *gotten spoils* 760 *[,] it*] , obscured by first stroke of *i* 761 Smudged erased letter under *g* of *good* indicates false start 762–5, 770 Speeches indented to differentiate verse from prose 764 *say*] *y* altered, ? from *s* 765 *the*] *t* altered from *o*; ? for *our* 767 *hearke*] *k* altered, ? from *e*

Rust: I cry you mercy sir I cannot hit yor court tearmes and what must I doe after I haue kist her.

Trist: why then you must vse yor best complements.

Rust. how must wee soe soone put in vre our implements.

Trist⟨.⟩ you are still wide for complementising is to speake the best phrase you can and vse the prettiest gestures you haue.

Rust: Troth I can[not] neyther breake iests nor vse phrases for I neuer tasted any since I came from Lincolne.

Trist: I see you are no thing intelligent.

Rust. Nay if I should bee negligent in these things I promise you I were much too blam⟨e⟩
oh how I wish to bee at court to congifie yor ladies, to complement yor gentlewomen, and to vse my best iests wth them both, but how shall I doe for phraises is there at court any egges and butter to make them? and may not I vse gesta Romanorū I thinke those are yor ancientst iests yt are.

Trist:⟨.⟩ Beshrow mee but heele much delight the king
h'ath wearied mee allready wth his chat
come lets away to horse braue RedRose knight [Fol. 13b]
weele see king Arthurs court ere wee see night. Exeunt.

Rust: Perhaps it may seeme strange to some are here
blunt Rusticano should in court appeare
but now and then some asses clad in gold
appeare in court [I] lesse prudent farre then bold. Ex.

Alaram. they crie within (king Arthur) then enter the king with a speare [with a speare] in his Rest as from the tilt, lords./

K: Tis tyme to leaue the lists./ not one appeares,
fifty choice knights this speare hath sent to th'earth
whence is that trumpet? Enter Androgeo { a trumpet sounds a farre of.

And: May it please yor grace
from farre appeare iiij comely knights in view
with gallant carriage riding ore the plaine
by this they are all enterd to the lists.

K: Prepare our courser, Guimiuer shall see
what for her beauty shall atcheeued bee. Ex.

Enter Gallowine Lancellot & Tristram in hast. Alaram.

Gall: oh see with what agility, hee makes
his braue curvetting courser for to mounte,
looke, now hee makes him bend his knee toth' queene,
and now braue Arthur and the sprightfull youth
doe cope together with like violence

797 *[I]*] altered before deletion 806 *lists*] ²*s* altered or retraced 807 *Guimiuer*] with nine minims and two dots
810 *makes*] *es* may be *s*

as when the waues and winds doe Rush together.
Lan: & see, they sitte both irremoueable
who would not honor thee braue Redrose knight?
Trist: And now behold againe they choose new staues, *A showte within./
& cannot stirre each other, *harke the voice
of the rude headed multitude doe shoute,
and echoes doe proclaime their fame
yet neither hath the best nor conquests name.
Gall: oh see their speares are sheeuered and they meete
like lyons in the shocke their horses feete
doe seeme to shake the earth, looke how they tugge,
And grapple each with other.
Lan: See the knight
doth plucke the king froms saddle by sterne might
harke, harke, againe they echoe foorth his fame. A shout wthin
T. The noyse soe shrill it seemes to moue earths frame
And here they come.

[MISSING] [FOL. 14a]

[MISSING] [FOL. 14b]

Toe Englands quondam kings, wee are borne free [FOL. 15a]
from servile bondage & base slau*er*y
further hee doth com̄aund in his name
to send him tribute wch if thou deniest
hee will orerunne thy land wth hostile armes
& foresee to it then preuent such harmes
K. Hee shall not need (Embassador/ weele rouse him
before hee thinke ont or expect our presence
Red: Shall I retourne an answere./
K. Doe bold spirit
Red⟨:⟩ Embassador returne vnto thy lord
tell him king Arthur hath such knights will daunt
the proudest hee that caused him to reuolt
looke to yor townes, & see them strongly guarded
for such an armie shall arriue in france

818 *choose*] ^{1}*o* added 823 *they*] *th* written over *mee* 828 *froms*] *from* altered from *to grou* (? for *to ground*) *saddle*] *ad* altered from *ed* *by*] *y* altered, ? from *ut*

Fol. 14 Only two small stubs remain, conjugate with Fol. 17, suggesting deliberate tearing out of leaf

832–3 Hand A 832 *free*] ^{2}*e* retraced or altered 833 *slauery*] *l* unusually short; first minim of *u* added

834–68 Hand D 834 *in*] ? for *thee in* 837 *foresee*] ? for *force*. *See*

sent from this Iland for to fright rebellion
as that false Leues shall tremble at the name
of conquering Arthur; for yor strongest forts
best guarded holds weele batter to the ground
when hartles Lewes yor king for dead shall sound
K. Begon thou hast thy message Ex. Em:
Red. oh my liege
(not ought detracting from these knights renowne)
create me generall of yor leuied Army
and Ile so startle base rebellious fRANCE
as shall thy fame and honor much aduaunce.
K. Seeing the stubborne Saxons still rebell
soe that wee cannot leaue our Realme wth safety
thy wishes second our desires; & wee
will cause great forces leuied speedily
bee y^{t} yor chardge S^{er} Gallowine
Gall It shall ⟨.⟩
looke to thy selfe (proud fRaunce) thou now shalt fall Ex.
K. Tristram Du-lionesse doe thou the like
& thou heroike Lancellot
Ambo so wee goe
prepare thy selfe (false france) wee see thy woe. Exeunt
Q: Is this yor page [Fol. 15b]
Red he is ant please yor grace
Q: he seemes to be a miery fellow is a not
Red he is renowned Queene
Q: Ile soone trie that, hearke yow fellow, Canst not heare,
come hither,
Rust: Now had I forgott all this while that I had bene in Court
to put in vse that wich sir Trimtram, what call yǒ him
did teach me, what a scurvy forgetfull asse am I, I a
Courtier I a dogstoord sireu*er*ens of the Company, well
nūquā sera est ad bonos mores via, the way to good man*er*s
is neu*er* to late & therefore Ile goe, (a pox ont, I am
a very rogue if I have[⟨.⟩]not forgott the word sir Tr.
tould me) Oh congity Ile een goe try my skill on
yander lady wich calls me [he runs and kisseth the queen]

851 *dead*] ? for *dread* 857 *aduaunce*] *c* heavily altered 860 *wee*] *w* and ^{2}e touched up in greyer ink 864 *fRaunce*] *c* altered 868 *Exeunt*] *x* altered from *e*

869–1283 Hand A 875 SP noticeably above line 877 *teach*] originally *tell*; ^{1}l deleted and *a* interlined above; ^{2}l altered to *c* by addition of *h* *scurvy*] *c* altered, ? from *r* *am*] mark above *a*, ? false start of *l* 878 *dogstoord*] *st* smudged 880 *late*] *l* altered from *t* 881 *Tr*] *r* altered from *ir* 883 *yander*] *a* ? misformed *o*

Q why how now sirrha
Kin: ha ha ha what hast thou don sirha, darste kisse my
wife before my face & not aske my leave first ha
Rust: I Cry yo^{w} hartily m*er*cy sir ist yor wife, Ile besworne
I did yt ingrauntly
Red: be ware sirha yts the queen yo^{w} may p*er*chaunce loose
yor head for this
Q: I like him well sweet Red rose suffer him a litle
Rust: It is the queen in troth I am the gladder onte, for
now when I goe to Lincolne what a grace will yt be
for me to say I kist the queens worship, pray p*ar*don
my Consumptuous dacity (fayre lady queen (was not this
good complementa$\overline{\text{con}}$⟨),⟩ in daringe to p*ro*stulat or touch
the mellow stincture, I wowld say tincture of yor
mellow dai⟨n.y⟩ red lips
Q why sirha whoe gave yo^{w} licence to kiss me
Russ: troth & yowle knowe the troth, the verity & sincerity of the
matter, myne owne mother witt, together with sir Trimt:
wise teachinge me to Curtesy ladies, made me soe bould as I was
King[Red]: Noe more here is sir Gallowine – soe soone returnde [en: Gall:
have yo^{w} accomplisht what yo^{w} had in charge
Gall: with all Celerity, and heare they stande
full thirty thowsand a most royall bande
K: Wee thanke yo^{w} Nephew, see the rest returnde
what power have yo^{w} levied
Ambo Thowsands stronge
to trifle thus they thinke yt ou*er* longe

enter sir Trist: & Laun:

⟨S⟩ [FOL. 16a]
⟨R⟩

⟨d⟩ry [FOL. 16b]
⟨.⟩ueld

I call thee where so ere thou art brave knight [FOL. 17a]
thy vallowre onely hath subdude our might

885 [1]*ha*] *a* altered from *oo* (? *hoo* = whoa) 889 *yo^{w}*] *w* altered from *r* 891 *Red*] *R* altered from *r* 892 *onte*] *o* retraced or altered 894 *worship*] flourish between *i* and *p*, ? false start for letter with looped ascender 895 *Consumptuous*] [1]*u* ? *e*; [2]*u* altered 896 *touch*] *c* altered, ? from *e* or *o* 897 *stincture*] *r* altered from *er* 898 *dai⟨n.y⟩ red*] interlined above caret 900 [1]*troth*] *r* altered from *h* 901 *Trimt*] *T* altered or blotted 905 *stande*] *t* altered, ? from *l* 906 *thirty*] *i* formed by dotting *r* 907 *Nephew*] *N* begun as *n* 909 *Ambo*] smudge above *A*

Fol. 16 Only small triangular stub at foot remains, conjugate with Fol. 15: surviving letters in Hand A

916 *thy*] *y* altered from *e*

where art thow Englands leader [enter Redrose k:
Red: Here I am, whoe art thow calst me
D:An: I am Aniows duke
Red: And I am hee thow seekest
Du: An: welcome thow art
Red: thowlt fynde other wyse ere we to p*ar*te
Alarū they fight; Red: kills duke An: Enter Duke of Guise
to his rescue he beats him in and exit [enter kinge of fraunce
Kf: O god the day is lost, and by the hand
only of him, whome noe man can wthstand
twise hath he beat me from my barbed steed
and nowe he ranges (like some chafed bore)
vnto the midst of our battalions
theres noe man can or dare abide his blowes
would he were here, the Redrose knight I call
whoe by his strength slayes & discomfits all
Alarū. enter Gallowine
Gall: Whoe calls the Red rose knight
k:f: tis I the kinge of nowe vnhappy fraunce
art thow the knight I faine would meet with
Gall: noe but yet will trie
wich best can weeld his weapon thee or I
Alarū they fight Gallowine beats him in, Enter Duke of Gwise
they fight, Enter duke Guise Gall: takes him prisoner
Exeunt,: enter Rusticano with a Clubb ins hands

Rus: O what a pietifull stirrs yonder, I thinke I have kild (doth noe body heare me) let me see, I have kilde and knocte downe at least forty and all mandfully behinde there backs, Oh what gallant lies will I tell when I goe home againe as how I haue kilde three at a blow, and thirty fightinge against onely one, I valeantly put them all to flight with nere a weapon in my hande with a thowsande more lies, but why doe I talke soe p*er*haps some man will see me wandring from my Company and soe knock out my braines, O lord I yeld, what a feare full rogue am I, to be soe fearefull of a dead body masse a was some noble man I warrant well Ile take him vp, and tell my m^r I have kilde him
[he offers to take him vp, then enter one of the ffrench peers & takes him prisoner, he cries out, then enter Launcelott & rescues him [FOL. 17b]

917 *Englands*] *a* blotted 918 *Here*] *H* altered from *h* 919 *Aniows*] *w* altered from *u* 922 *wyse*] *y* altered from *i* 923 Pen mended 924 *fraunce*] *c* retraced or altered 938 *weapon*] *e* altered, ? from *a* 939 *in*] *i* altered, ? from start of *h* 943 ²*me*] *m* has four minims *downe*] *n* altered from *e* 944 *all*] interlined above caret

and taks him prisoner, then enter other peers and fight with
sir Launcelott, he is like to be slayne: Alarum: enter sir
Tristrā: he fighteth with them they two take all the peers
prison*er*s and Exeunt: Alarum Enter kinge of ffraunce & Red:
they fight Red rose knight takes him prison*er* Exeunt: Enter
Rust: Peers call y^{w}them I neu*er* saw such pears in all my life, they
are not like our pears in England, for I can eat twentie
of them together, and I thinke on my troth one of these ffrench Pears will eat
twenty of me, I can put a hundred of our pears in my two pockets, whereas
one of these ffrench pears are as bigge as my selfe: Nay wich is the greatest
marvayle: nay wich is a greater matter: on of these pears was like
to kill me: whereas I have eaten forty of our pears in the sum̄*er* time,
and have bene neu*er* a whit the worse: but see the peers are fallen
and here comes our noble generall, with all our enimies vanquisht
A floorish enter Red: and all his hoast, leadinge the ffrench kinge and
all his prisoners
Red: first thanks to heaven, nexte vnto y^{r} power
By whome wee victors are this happy hower
Disloyall to thy sou*er*aigne nowe thou seest
the iust rewarde of hated piury
yet weel not triumph ou*er* misery
Thow arte the cause p*ro*ducinge these effects
many a thowsande now a pray to death
hadst thow bene Loyall had enioyde theyr breath
K f: With horrowre I Confesse yt, penitence
somewhat though litle lesson the offence
Red yt doth in deed and Arthure yow shall see
(repentaunce had) will p*ar*don willingly
Rust: Doe ye heare m^{r} will you graunt me on request for
all the service I have done yow in these warrs
Red speake one wee giue yt freely
Rust: Why sir I would haue some forty of those french pears to send for
tokens to our friends in England, they will wonder to see such great ones
Trist: Thow mistakest thy selfe man⟨;⟩ these pears are lords
Rust: I wowld I were one two, soe I might be a lord, but doe yow
heare sir Trimtram as brave as they be were they in wooster
shire they wowld quickly be layde hands one, for there they love
pears out of all cesse & measure

957 *Launcelott,*] , obscured by *f* in *fighteth* below *slayne*] *l* altered, ? from *h* *Alarum*] *l* altered from *a* 958 *fighteth*] ^{2}*t* formed as *f* 961 *Peers*] *P* altered from *p* 962 Pen mended 963 ^{2}*of*] *o* altered 966 *on*] *o* altered or retraced *pears*] *r* altered from *s* *was*] *w* altered from *t* 972 *Red*] *R* altered from *K* 975 *piury*] ? for *periury* 976 *triumph*] *t* altered from *c* Vertical mark after *misery* is flaw in paper 981 *lesson*] *on* altered or blotted 991 *heare*] *h* altered from long *s*

Red Well Countrey men and hardy followers [FoL. 18a]
whoe soe amongst yo̅ by his mighty hand
hath conquered any worthy of this land
his ransomes freely at his owne dispose
he merits best that Conquers Countreys foes
french kinge & pears of fraunce, yow all must hence
Captiue to Arthure happy Englands prince
Away to sea, England when once wee meete
thy browes wth most viclorious Palmes weel greete
Come fellow sowldiers
Omnes when the ffrench rebell
Thus lett the brittaines theyre prowde fury quell [Exeunt om:
Enter Time as Chorus
Time Time is not lost when time in time, returnes,
Tyme yet intreats yow stay some longer time
to see what powerfull Acts brave Arthurs sonne
shall yeat accomplish: wherefore let yor thoughts
safely Conducte him backe, on Englands shore
wth all the trophies of his victories
yt both shall feed yor eares and please yor eyes [exit Time]
A florish Enter Red: Gallo: Laun: Trist: wth theyre Captives
Red: Hayle Englande thus I resalute thy browe
(as ioyfull of our salph reviwe of thee
with lawrell branches signe of victory
nowe welcome Countreymen: nay welcome all
Grieve not yow frenchmen at yor soddayne fall
Arthure is milde & yow must yeld to fates
yow penitent he will restore yor states
K.f. let Heaven witness of our penitence
and harty sorrowe for our great offence
Red then tis sufficient: how now messenger [Enter Messenger]
Mess: His Royall maiesty brave generall
attended wth a royall trowpe of horse
Comes to congratulate yor salph returne
and see they enter
Sounde Enter kinge Arthure, Queen Gwiniu*er*: Androgeo: Lords
K: Rise famowse yowth that makste myne honowre rise
higher then fames imblazonde tongue can rayse yt
thy p̄rsent salfa returne with victory
returns to Arthures Court all royalty

994 *followers*] [1]*l* altered from *o* 1012 *his*] *is* altered, ? from *e* 1014 *A florish*] added by A after rest of line was written
Captives] *iv* formed as *w* and dotted 1016 *salph*] *p* altered, ? from *h*

Q: My prayers now have had a ioyfull ende
Welcome to Englands Court our dearest friend
Rust: And shall I have nere a welcome home, nowe looke on [Fol. 18b]
me and yow will, I am Rusticano that once stole a kisse
of yow, for wich I prsent yow with two of the greatest pears
yow eu*er* sawe or tasted in all yor life
Qu: where are they good fellowe
Rus: these french outlandish fruite
Q dost meane these lords wich are captives
Rust: I those Captious lords
Qu. Goe to, got to, thow art a miery fellow
Ru: Nay yf yf yow had seen me lay about me in fraunce
yow would haue sworne I had bene a mad fellow
Red: Madam I humbly Crave yor princely hand
Qu: with all our heart (renoned brittaine)
Red Great kinge behould the gou*er*nowre
vnder yor mats of now Conquered ffraunce
see heare the duke of Guise thus Captive led
see heare the pears of ffraunce thus Conquered
Ru: And see heer Rusticano Conqueroure
K: A: most Loyall subiects Arthure thanks yow all
for worthy service done yor kinge and Countrey
and know that Arthure neu*er* will forgett
the rare Acheevemts wich yow have p*er*formde
devide the spoyles amonge you and returne
vnto yor wives wich much yor absence mourne
L Thy subiects p*ro*mise for thy love, great lord
to fight for thee wth hand, wth hart, with sword
K: A: but now to thee prayse worthy generall
what can I yeld thee equall to thy merits
arte: will engrave thy name in Annales pende
vntill æternity shall have an ende
Red Cease mighty prince oh stop yor theame of prayse
of such a worthy subect, let me crave one boon
for all my service
Kin: A: speake and have
R tis not for wealth the misers sacred god

1034 *prayers*] ²*r* altered from *s* 1036 *I*] followed by false start for further letter *nowe*] *ow* altered, ? from *op* 1037 *me and*] *m* and *nd* heavily inked or blotted 1039 *yow*] *y* altered or smudged 1042 *lords*] *s* altered, ? from *d* 1045 *yf yf*] ? for *yf yt* ²*me*] *m* has four minims 1049 *behould*] *h* altered or blotted 1055 *service*] *c* altered, ? from long *s* 1060 *Thy*] *y* altered from *e* 1063 *yeld*] *l* altered from *e* 1065 *æternity*] *æ* altered from *e* 1067 *a worthy*] ? for *vnworthy* *crave*] *r* altered, ? from *a* 1070 *for*] *f* altered from *w*

nor for ambition lofty myndes doe ayme at
Nor yet for lands (the rusticks demy god [FOL. 19a]
neither for livinge of some statefallen men
(as courtiers vse doe sue, beg or crave
the s$\overline{\text{ome}}$ is this: I knowe I have some father
but whoe, or where is that know I not:
him will I seeke: in seekinge whome thy [arme] name
this arme shall sownd foorth and p*ro*clayme thy fame

K Tis bootles to disswade thy firm resolve
Cowld I recall my words thow showldst not goe
but kinges most neu*er* violat theyr p*ro*mise
neither will I adewe brave Tom a Lincolne
Let fortune eu*er* lacky by thy side
auspicious vertue eu*er* be thy guide

Ga:L:T: wee vowe to follow thee where ere thy starrs
shall s⟨a⟩lfe conducte thee, neu*er* will we three
p*ar*te from thine eu*er* blessed Company

Red: I Can but thanke yo^{w} all, now mighty lord
thus humbly on my knees I take my leave
lament not for our absence wee must hence
Nature bids goe, yor kindenes stay (great prince)
by Gods asistans wee will safe returne:
nexte famowse princes, & my sou*er*aign queene
I leve yor grace, whose grace my ioy hath bene
Captives of ffraunce we bid yo^{w} all farewell
more should I speake, myne eyes with tears would swell

Rust:
Nowe must I take my leave to, farewell good m^{r}kinge Karter, & m^{rs} queen Miniver, and all yo^{w} french pears, if I could take yo^{w} wth me yo^{w} should come alonge thats flatte, for yo^{w} know travellers have good stommacks, and would be gladde of a peare to quench there thirst sometimes I could whine for very anger to thinke I must leave such good company: o lo lo lo lord, I must lea. le le leave my fellowe Courtiers theres noe remnant

G: L: T: Thy lovinge subiects eu*er* pray thy grac^{e}
may eu*er* flourish, till we reviwe this plac^{e}

K f: Th[e]y rare acheevem^{ts} fortune still attende
and bringe thy wishes to an happy end

1076 *or*] *o* formed as *v* *where*] ? for *where he* 1077 *thy*] *y* altered from *i* at same time as substitution of *name* for *arme*
1079 *disswade*] *d* altered from *e* *firm*] *i* formed by dotting *r* 1083 *thy*] *t* altered, ? from long *s* 1088 *yo^{w}*] *o* blotted
1092 *returne*] ^{1}*r* altered, ? from *h* 1094 *leve*] *e* altered from *a* *yor*] *y* altered from *g* 1108 *bringe*] *in* has four minims

[Fol. 19b]

Red: Aboord Companions launch vnto the deepe
Heaven thine happy state, blesse, saue, & keepe [Exit Red & his Company]

King A: see they are gone Come lett vs in to sporte
fraunce shall knowe, Arthure keepes a princely Corte [Exeunt omnes]

Enter time

Time Can not longe be absent, least yo^{w} stray
and now should loose the Brittaines by the way
to whome milde Neptune & the powers of sea
six years together p*ro*ved gently Calme
In wich theyre navigation, they fore past
Many a monarchs Court & potentate
Coastinge ore Spaine and frutefull Italy
Europ & TurKey, wth great Affrica
In wich stands auncient Carthage; Barbary
Numidia, Mauritania, wich is p*ar*ted
In Tyngitania, that hath one the west
The Curled Ocian, on the north the straights
of stowte Morocco sowth——Getulia
Cæsariensis—Mauritania hath
the sea Sardoū leaninge to the North
the mountayn Libia bendinge to the sowth
ye all the spacious orbe he and his mates
had well nigh Coasted, Countreys, kingedomes, states
all, ye all, yet neu*er* coulde he heare
the least suspition of his longe sought sire
but left behinde him still a glorious fame
of the rownd table and of Arthures name
Nowe at the end of six years Navigation
they have descride a very famowse lande
where how they spedde yo^{w} p^{r}sently shall heare
yf yo^{w} but lende them an atentive eare EXIt

Enter Red: Gall: Laun: Trist: a mariner, & Rusticano

Red vpon what shore are we arived speake
what Countrey[.] doe we tread one?

Mar: fayry lande,
they say noe men inhabit heare, if soe
nought can wee looke for but deiected woe/

1112 *princely*] *l* altered   1118 *fore*] ? for *ore*   1130 *mates*] *e* altered from *s*   1132 *ye*] *y* altered from *l*
1140 *Enter*] *e* blotted   1141 *arived*] *iv* altered from *o*   1143 *fayry*] *a* altered from *i*   1144 *men*] *m* has four minims
if] *f* altered, ? from long *s*   1145 *woe*] *w* altered or blotted

Rust: woe (quotha), if there can be greater woe then wee [FOL. 20a]
suffer, I much m*ar*vayle, for Ile besworne I am almost fanished
for want of some victualls, I have eat nothinge these fowre⟨r⟩
dayes, and now my gutts keepe such a squablinge in my belly
as I feare they will fall in a mutinie amonge them selves
and soe run out of my mowth: O lorde now can I not but
remember, the many gawnes of poridge I have eaten
at my fathers in Lincolne, the good worts & Cabages we
were wonte to have vpon Tewsedayes & [Thudaes]
thorsdayes at supp*er*, the good martlemas beife and bacon
as yellowe as the gowlden noble, wee were vsed to have
vpon sondayes & holly dayes: ah Mother Sisley, mother
sisly, thow wast wont to sweare I was sicke, If I went
but thrise [of⟨.⟩] a dinner to the poredge pott, alas, alas,
that eu*er* I left thee to dy a dogges death
Tri: [L] Let come what will weel stand thus opposite
To ominous fates, and fortunes greatest spight
Can wee but fill vs
Gall: how can wee doe ill
If yo^{w} cælestiall powers will aide vs still
Red: But Mariner how can yt be that men
rule not this lande: can there be woemen then
Mar: They can and thus yt was, not many years are past
since that a famowse and renowned prince
raignde ore this kingedome (Calde the fayry knight⟨)⟩
whoe waginge warre against a neighbor kinge
eight years together left the fayry lande
be refte of men, now the faerian dames.
longing for that wich woemen most desire
there nightly sport and wished dallians
sent for theyre howsebands backe: whoe thus returne
theyre wives an answer: bid them be Content
and wee will see them at this warrs event
there wives impatient at this sterne reply
vowde that theyre howsebands at returne showlde dy
and beinge come home victors, as they greed
each in theyre beds did make there howsebands bleed

1146 *(quotha),*] *(* retraced; *)* obscures , 1147 *suffer*] blot between ^{2}f and *e* *for*] *r* retraced or altered from *e* 1151 *can*] *ca* altered from *no* 1154 *Thudaes*] *Thu* altered from *fri*; *e* ? from *i* 1159 *poredge*] *p* altered 1161 *[L]* false start 1165 *powers*] *r* altered from *s* 1168 *They*] ? for *There* *years*] *y* altered or smudged 1172 *eight*] *e* altered from *y* 1177 *wives*] *v* altered from long *s* 1178 *event*] *v* altered

Onely the kinges bright daughter in a boate
did put her father in the seas to float
and eu*er* since hath Cælia bene queene
as instantly to all y^{t} shalbe seene

[enter 2 Ladies wth bowes & arrows in theyr hands and quiu*er*s or thwart theyre backs] [FOL. 20b]

Red O irreligious acte: see where they Come
i L Our royall queene Comāunds yo^{w} in her name
(like base in truders as yo^{w} are) relurne
vnto yor tottered shipps what madnes Causde yow
to enter thus our confines: nere was seene
a man app*ere* vpon this goodly greene
these many yeares together: hence away
fly to yor ships theres danger in delay
Red: fayre Lady to yor queen returne vs thus
tell her that Brittish men: & traveloures
desiere some succour from her: whoe denies
either weel slay them or our honowre dies
returne with speedy answer
i Lady wee desire
Our queene may yeld to thys yo^{w} doe requier [Exe:
La: if she refuse, by heaven weel with stand
her & her forces, had she Xerxes bande
Tris: May Tristrams arme, ner̂e more wield branded sword
but weel glutt hunger ere we goe aboorde
Red: have any of yo^{w} seene the queen
Mar: I have they are soe huge a fæmal multitude
as that without amazem^{t} non can tell
each beares a bendinge bow, & p*er*cinge shafte
with each a quiu*er* ou*er* thwart theyre backs
thus goe they still like fayre Dianas trayne
Chasinge the stagge, but see they turne againe
Gall in fayth thy are gallant wenches
i La: save yow lords
The queen of fayeries sends yo^{w} answer thus
either yo^{w} must returne, or with our shafts
weel quickly pearce yor bosomes (tied fast
vnto some senceles oake: or Come with vs
to Cælia fayry queene: to bide her doome
one of these to (choose either) must be done

1185 *hath*] ^{1}h altered, ? from *b* 1186 *shalbe*] *h* altered from *l* *or thwart*] loop between *h* and *w* may be vestigial *o* 1187 *see where*] words nearly linked by *u*-formed loop between ^{2}e and *w* 1202 *by*] *y* altered from *e* 1207 *fæmal*] *æ* blotted or altered *multitude*] *it* altered from *u*; ^{2}t uncrossed 1209 *percinge*] *per* abbreviation altered from *pro* abbreviation 1211 *Dianas*] *D* altered from *d* 1213 *fayth*] *a* altered from *e* *thy*] ? for *they* 1216 *must*] *u* altered from *os*

Red: Resolved we goe: that ere we dy wee sweare [FOL. 21a]
Our p^{r}cious lives, weel rate, & prize full deare

Rus: Nowe whats best for me to doe, if I stay heare then shall not I be shott
to death by yonder fayries: If I goe yander then shall I not die
heare for want of victualls: but on both sides heres nothing but death
to be expected, Is yt not a pittifull case m^{rs}, that such a hope=
full yonge man as my selfe, showld be cast away at these years
I thinke yt the best way to p^{r}vent daunger & these tripping
fayeryes even to knock out my owne braynes: Nay
birlady for a body might be accessary of his owne death
but I marvayle what this queene of fayries is: p*er*haps yts
shee that putteth money in mens shoos in the night time
if yt be she I hope sheel p*ar*done me for my mothers sake
whoe would neu*er* goe to bed a nights, but shee would have
the howse cleane swepte: the ashes cleane rakte vp
in the Chimney harth: a boowle of water and a cleane
towell layde vpon the bench: vnder the skreem & all
this shee sayde, was for the queene of fayries & her green⟨e⟩
Coat Company: and eu*er*y morninge continually she
would finde money in the bowle, in wich the water
was in: One night above the rest: I listned about
twelve a clocke at night: to see if I could here thē
and me thoughts I hard the sweetest bells ringe I
heard in my life: but see I have taulked soe longe
of them that I had almost forgott my selfe: well
ingens Telum necessitas: I must goe p*er*force for
hunger Constraines me: and if I dy yt is some
Comnfort to dy with Company: solamen miseris socios
habuisse dolores: wherefore Ile euen after them
as fast as I can [Exit]

Sounde: enter Cælia the fayry queene with ladies attending
her: having bowes and arrows in there hands: & quivers &c

1 La: I assure yo^{w} madam [I]eie nere saw
more goodly featurde or demenurde knights
they stile themselves knights of kinge Arthures Cort
the Brittaine Monarch: whose prayes fame reports
theyre resolution and theyre mynds soe rare
as that in my conceyt yts past compare

1223 *stay*] *y* retraced or altered 1231 *marvayle*] *l* altered, ? from *e* 1232 *shoos*] ²*s* altered, ? from *l* 1234 ²*would*] *o* altered, ? from *u* 1236 *boowle*] ²*o* blotted 1237 *skreem*] *m*, ? *ne* 1244 *taulked*] *u* altered or retraced; *k* altered from *d* 1249 *euen*] ²*e* altered from *er* suspension 1250 ¹*as*] *s* added 1252 *her*] *r* added, or retraced *hands*] *nd* altered from amalgamated *nd* form 1256 *Monarch*] otiose flourish over *c*

Qu: what sondry passions doe aflict mynde
are they soe resolute & yet soe kinde
1 La: They are, now lett yor ey⟨e⟩s be yor ow⟨ne⟩ iudges
see where they are

enter Red & his Company [Fol. 21b]

Q O imortall gods asside
what have yov placte all yor rarest guifts
here in one princely yowth: ore are yor selves
Come downe assuminge this our ftraylest nature
to make me be enamord of yor p*er*sons
but peace noe more: hayle Curteous Champions
Red Thanks Amazonian: we are come to try .
whether yowle sucker our extremity
if I: thus lowe we bend: if noe by might
bowldly wee[l] will confront yor greatest might
Gall: Armde with vndaunted spirits thus we stand
In bowld defians of yor maiden band
La: And thus resolv̂d weel cloy o[r]r appetite
with yor relentles flesh by valowre myght
Tr: And if lyke Caniballs yow thirst for bloud
Wee rate ors deare to bwy yt wer[t]not good
Ru: Now must I say somethinge to fright them the more, nay
if yow medle wth vs we will hew yow smaller then hearbs
in the potte, we are p*er*ills fellowes I can tell yow if we
be angred, and Ile be sworne I had neu*er* a better stomack
in all my life,: then I haue now, but I faith tis
to eate &[c] not to fight,/Aside
yet be no more then barbaro*us*, O see
and seeing, pitty our calamity.
Q. I cannot cast mine eies from off his sight, Asyde
they yeeld me such vnspeakeable delights;
braue Christians; you mistake vs, take repose
for ever in our land, as frinds, not foes
be Iovial Ioyfull frolik what Content
these place can yeld ye take with all assent
Ladies pr̃pare a sumptuous banquett goe Exe: la:
weel turne to mirth yor misconceaved woe

1259 *mynde*] ? for *my mynde* 1264 *yor*] *r* ? altered 1265 *here*] *h* altered from *y* *princely*] *r* altered from *l* 1268 *but*] *b* altered from *p* and smudged 1270 *sucker*] *ck* altered from *ff* *extremity*] *r* altered from *e* 1271 *noe*] *e*, ? *r* 1272 *will*] interlined above deletion with caret 1274 *maiden*] *m* altered 1275 *cloy*] *y* altered, ? from *s* 1276 *flesh*] *fl* altered 1277 *lyke*] *ly* altered from *y* 1278 *Wee*] *W* altered, ? from *f* or long *s* 1279 *Ru*] *R* smudged

1283–90 Hand E: from *then I haue* 1284 Slash before *Aside* cuts through , 1285 *no*] ? for *not* *O*] altered, ? from long *s* 1290 *foes*] *e* ? retraced or altered

1291–1473 Hand A 1292 *these*] ? for *this* 1293 *Exe* :] *e* written over original *:* , *:* rewritten 1294 *misconceaved*] 2*c* ? altered from long *s*

Ru: O there spake an Angell: my very bowells lepte wthin me at [FoL. 22a]
that sweet word, $\overset{r}{p}$pare a banquett observe the words: not
deferre nor delay tell some other time, but $\overset{r}{p}$pare, make ready
wth all speede not a clownicall dinner. of poodinge & bacon
not a rusticall supp*er* of p*ar*senipes & Carets, but a banquette
$\overset{r}{p}$pare a banquett, not onely soe but a sumptuous, a Costly
a daynty delicat banquett: $\overset{r}{p}$pare a sumptuous banquett⟨?⟩
Oh how I could still meditate one these words: methinks I
have fild my belly wth the conceyt of soe admirable wordes
$\overset{r}{p}$pare a sumptuous banquett:

Red: Wee all are silent for wee cannot give
yor kindenes thanks sufficient while we live

Qu: How sweet is eu*ery* accent of his speech
Composde and grac'te wth liuely Rhetoricke
Come prethy sit downe by me: Come y$\overset{r}{o}$ hand
In fayth I will not sitt if yo^{w} doe stande

Red: It ill befitts me Madam

Q fayth yo^{w} shall
Poore Cælia he hath wonne thine hart and all asyde
I burne I burne sweet modesty repell
those scorching flames wthin me worse then Hell
Why art disconsolate, be frolick man
mirth fitts the tyme

Red Bright princesse soe I am

Ru: And I am horrible an hungry: I thinke in my Consciens I
could eat more puddinge then eu*er* steeven Hide did: but
noe more, heare comes the banquett: I can forbe⟨a⟩re no longer
the banquett is brought in musicke: Rusticano takes a whore
dish of sweet meats, and throws into his mouth by handfulls

Red: How now sirha be more manerly

Que: Let the fellow alone sweet knight for hees hungry

Ru: troth and soe I am queen of fayries: and hunger cares not for com=
plen^{ts}: soe yt may have inough to fills panch withall: I remember a
true verse since I went to schoole: fames malū quo non alius
velocius vllū: the meaninge of the verse is this: that hunger
is euill and that theres nothinge more swifte quick & nimble, y^{t}
yt is evill I have had a prety triall these two or three dayes
and that yt is quick or nimble yo^{w} see yt by exp*er*iens, for my
hande was first in the dish

1308 *liuely*] *e* altered from fourth minim of *iue* 1309 *prethy*] *e* altered or blotted 1319 *thinke*] *k* altered or blotted 1322 *whore*] ? for *whole* 1325 *Que* :] altered from *Om.* 1328 *to*] altered, ? from long *so* *schoole*] *c* altered from *h* 1329 *is*] *s* altered from *t* 1330 *euill*] *ill* altered from *er* suspension and smudged 1331 *had*] *h* altered from *y* 1333 *first*] *i* formed as *r* but dotted

La: thow dost abuse the verse man yts fama not fames
Ru: but I say yts fames not fama, yowle graunt me yts spoken
of fames yf yt be not of fama will yow not
La: I will
Ru: Well then: theres somethinge more swift then fame ergo yts
not spoken of fame
La: I deny yor p^{r}cedent
Ru: Precedent; yow must say antecedent, as wee schollers doe
La: They doe but verbally differ
Ru: Sic p*ro*bo, theres somethinge more swifte then fame, thus I p*ro*ve
yt; a woomans tongue is more swifte then fame, but a
woomans tongue is something ergo thers something
more swifte then fame: what can yo^{w} denye if the
maior: why all men howld yt to be the swiftest thinge
In the world, And I am sure ont twill ly faster then eu*er* fame
did
L I gr⟨a⟩unt yo^{w} the best Concedo, concedo/
Ru: Yo^{w} can not choose for the maior is impugnable, vnlesse (with the
Collier yo^{w} showld deny my Conclusion
Q. Sit downe, sit downe see iollity attends
thy selfe sweete brittayne, and thy lovely friends
Drinke, Come Carowse full healths about the boord
Thus I begin let musick lowde be sownde
whilst to this brittayne knight I drinke p*ro*found
Red: Thus, I receave yt, gieving yt agayne
to yo^{w} bright lady
1 Lady I can not refrayne
Our Queen imposde yt, and I thus retort, this to the next
Gall: I thanke yo^{w} madam forte,
I thus accepte yt, and (for tis a rownde
the lady nexte yo^{w} wth this Cup Ile wound
Ru: wowld yt were come to me my mouth waterse at yt
2 Lady: Thus Ile retort yt heare brave knight to yo^{w}
L: I kindely take yt for tis my due
but here yt shall not rest rownde yt must goe
Lady yo^{w}le pleadge me,
3 Lady: How can I say noe
yo^{w} are the last, and soe with yo^{w} yt ends

1335 *yowle*] *w* ? altered *spoken*] *p* ? altered 1336 *yf*] *f* altered from *t* [1]*not*] *t* altered from *c* 1341 *antecedent*] [2]*t* altered from *d* 1343 *swifte*] *e* altered from *s* 1345 *ergo*] *r* altered or retraced; *o* ? altered from *oe* 1348 Darker ink and mended pen from *, And I* suggesting fresh start after interruption *And*] *A* altered from *I* *faster*] *s* altered from *t* 1350 *gr⟨a⟩unt*] *a* blotted and altered *concedo*] [1]*c* altered from *d* 1358 *Thus,*] *,* falls very low, under *s* 1359 *bright*] second stroke of *g* dotted 1360 *Lady*] added *y* obscures original *:* 1364 *lady*] *l* altered, ? from start of *n*

Tr: Madam with me truly⟨,⟩ Ile make amends
vnder yor favoure drinkinge to yor grace
Q Good knight yor offered kindenes I embrace [Fol. 23a]
Ru: Embrace say yo^{w} I would I could once embrace the cup
with my hands: heres nothinge but tossinge of whole ones
but still the cup passes ore Poore Rusticanos nose: Nay
Ile besworne they doe not leave as much as a snuffe
Q: Well honest friend thes health I drink to thee
Ru: Wich to requite I vowe to tosse of three (he drinketh iij^{es}
theyre lawe, I thought I showld neu*er* quench my thirst, but
one cannot doe a good thinge to ofte: and therefore Ile saye yt
once more: ô tis admirable good liquor: ô that all the water
in the sea were such, then twere good travelinge by water
but Ile goe aske the queen of fayry one thinge: Are not yow
that queen of fayries wich the ould songe speaks of in this man*er*
the queene her name was mob, wich through a wall of brasse
and through the centers of the earth: shee could most swiftly passe
if yow be I marvayle when wee shall see and yor green
Coat Company dauncinge on midsom*er*s eeve: on my troth if we
might see yo^{w} at lincolne, weed have for yo^{w} a cuppe of the best
ale could be gotten for love or money
Q sweet knight⟨s⟩ fall to yo^{w} see yor entertayne
Omnes thanks beloved queene
Q Ladies p*re*sent there eares
wth love strayndе Harmony most like the sphears
A songe
Come fayre Ceres, Lovely Venus
Come be p^{r}sent at our feasts
Come God Bachus, Come Sylenus
Entertayne these princely guests
with mirthfull haes
with rowndelayes
with ravisht kisses [Comely]
Comely graces
With sweet desiers, with Cupids fires
with armes enfowldinge hearts embraces
Brave Brittaynes Cheare, ye are welcome heare
Our virgins treasures open to yow

1372 *make*] *e* altered from *s* 1373 *favoure*] *e* added 1376 *nothinge*] *h* altered from *t* 1379 *thes*] *es* blotted 1385 *thinge*] *g* altered, ? from *k* 1389 *see*] ? for *see you* 1390 [1] *on*] small mark over *n*, presumably false start *midsomers*] *s* unclear, could result from blot on final stroke of suspension 1401 *guests*] *u* altered from *e* 1402 *mirthfull*] *f* altered from *l* 1403 *rowndelayes*] *a* altered from *o* 1409 *open*] dot within *o* (as in majuscule form)

The caske vnlocke, the lids a smocke
such sweet, sweet theffe can nere vndo yo^{w}
Bachus Let not wine be wantinge [Fol. 23b]
Ceres takake not plenty hence
Cupid with thine arrowes vaunting
strike vs for our great offence
Too too longe, ŵ have done the wronge
our maiden heads p*er*plex vs sore
forgive vs this, weel Clip, weel kisse
and neu*er* thus offende thee more
Brave &c
Venus p*ar*done oer offences
Venus wee are onely thine
our eyes, our ears, our hearts our sences
still adore thy sacred shrine
Rich pearles not vsde: or much abusde
men say our mayden heads are soe
then ere they rust, yo^{w} knights we trust
will Cleare our pearles before we goe
Brave Brittaines cheer &c
But why doe wee delay the time thus
deeds are better farr then words
If we offend because wee rime thus
wound vs wth yor pleasing swords
I meane those darts, wich wounde maids hearts
yet neu*er* can orcome them quite
away wth blowes, keepe them for foes
our onely fightings in the night
Brave Brittaynes Cheare, yare welcome heare
Our virgins treasures open to yow
The Caske vnlock, the lids a smocke
Such sweet sweet thefte can nere vndo yo^{w}
Q: subdude, subdude poore Captive as I am Asyde
by this renowned gallant Brittish man
venus if wee adore thee shew yt now
make his heart bende as thou hast made myne bow
How please our sports
Red: how can they ought displease
musicks to griefe a solace, to payne eas

1417 *vs*] round *s* altered from long *s* 1418 *kisse*] *is* altered from *u* 1425 *or*] ? for *are* 1431 *farr*] ^{2}r altered from *e* 1438 *Brittaynes*] *B* altered from *b* 1439 *treasures*] ^{2}r altered from *s* 1440 *Caske*] *C* altered from long *s* *smocke*] small stroke like apostrophe over *c* 1447 *Red*] *R* altered from *K*

Gall: why what man breaths there (if sence speaks him man)
but would be ravisht with these lofty straynes
these Cyrens risinge fallinge warblinge notes
these oh I can not finde an epithite
for to expresse Cælestiall musicks hight

Ru: yow know noe more what yo^{w} talke one, then this pott doth let me hau⟨e⟩ [FOL. 24a]
a can of Nappy ale, & tom pip*er* of Lincolne and I wil stand to yt
tis better then all yor louts ar barne doores what soeu*er*

Red: My man hath washt away his witts in beere

Ru: I marvayle yow^{l} offer to talke soe with a good fellow, yo^{w} thinke I am
dronke, but by this good beare/ he drinks/ I am æs sober as as as
yor greatest puritan in Banbury, nor doe not thinke Ile take
this abuse at yor hands, by this beare /he drinks/ I will not put
yt vp, Tapster bring in the other haulfe dozen, here, yo^{w} thinke
I can not stand, but doe not I stande as well as the best heare
/He falls/ sa ho when will this rascally Tapster come, why boy I say
so ho Chamberlaine. I am a very rogue but a litle thing, would
make me———He falls a sleepe

Qu: soe nowe hees fast, Ladies goe fetch some lights
to guide these knights vnto theyre wisht for rest
I knowe theyre weary limbes are ou*er* toylde
softe beds shall eas them, soe good night to all
this night ile bed with thee what ere befall———Asyde

Red: the like we wish to yo^{w} and all yor trayne

Q: nought but thy love can eas myne Ætna payne—Asyde

Rusticano talkes in his sleepe. Exeunt omnes

a good fellowes a good fellow in any place in England puh hang vp all those base roges w^{ch}
will not bee drunke in good companie troth queene mob I can eate no more at this tyme
is this a softest bed yo^{u} can affoord strangers and trauelers by my fayth my bones ake with
hardnes of my lodging must wee to sea so soone wth a vengeance wee shall neuer haue done
till wee bee either famished starued or drowned o lord blesse vs Iesus I thinke the
worlds at an end looke how the waues tosse and tumble wee are all cast away all cast
away help help help hold hold hold some one to the sterne of the shippe looke to the tack
ling of the ship all my freinds in Lincolne farewell now now now oh oh oh {hee
am I not dead let mee see o god I was neuer in such a pittifull dreame since my riseth}
name was Rusticano meethinkes all wee knights of the round table bee drowned at a
clap, but softe where am I trow, and where all my companie what is it night or doe
I still dreame, now cannot I tell whether I am still in a dreame or being drowned

1450 *straynes*] *t* altered from *c* 1451 *warblinge*] *in* altered or blotted 1453 *hight*] *ig* altered, ? from *ug* 1454 *doth*] *d* altered from *b* *hau⟨e⟩*] *u* blotted; *e* uncertain 1456 *tis*] *t* altered *ar*] ? for *or* 1463 *heare*] first stroke of *h* extended over *ear* by slip of pen 1465 *Chamberlaine*] *h* altered from *y*

1474–93 Hand D except *Exeunt omnes*, 1474, added by Hand A 1477 *trauelers*] *l* altered, ? from *e* *fayth*] *f* altered from *b* 1482 3*now*] final flourish of *w* extends to stage direction 1485 *trow*] *t* altered from *c*

in the bottome of the sea I am in another darke world god I grace I am not in pur
gatory it is soe darke what doe I feele (hee takes vp the pot) sure it is the soule
of some poore man in purgatorie that had not money to giue the popes worship to free
him out of purgatory but stay it feeles like a pot p*er*haps tis a pot of S^{t} francis to carry
soules ot purgatory o (now I know tis the pot wch I dranke in lately, well I am now
come to my selfe, I will goe seeke my m^{r} and the rest of my fellow knights god grant
I and the ladies bee faste tuckt together, Ile make and they bee thats flatte

Enter 2 saylers — But twoe of our saylers come, what is theyr busines, trowe not to goe [FOL. 24b]
to sea so soone I hope, for I haue not well disgested my late Rumbeling
yet, well Ile heare what they say:

first say — O Rustcano good morowe, good day Rusticano

[first]Rust: — Good day why? it not day yet

1. say: — Not wth this world, but it is wth thee, for thou has lately beene in an
other world, in an other hemispheare, in an other region, our gen*er*all
the Red Rose knight hath sent vs to knowe how thou doost. for knowing
of thy late typsines. he feares some evill should betyde thee,

Rust: — How typsines? Ile proue, (that I will/ him to be noe good fellowe, (noe
honest man that nowe & [will] then will not be kadumbeld wth his
friend & because I Canot proue wth sownd reason therefore Ile
sing it most hyperbolically & thus Ile begin

A songe:

Roome for a boone Companion
A braue & iouiall hangman
whoe loues to be drunke, who loues well a puncke
And as well the pitcher will bang man
And. still he roares. for some ale, for some lickour
o for some rich Tobacco
He raves & sings & heavens vaults rings
As long as of beere there is noe lacke ho:
yor drunkard is a lawyer
there is none thats heere but knowe him
his clients the pot wch he soakes god wot
& empty away he throwes it
And still he roares &^{c}.
yor drunkards a physitian
ingredienc^{e} he hath at his will sr
beare ale & smoake, doe vomits prouoke
& many he often doth kill sir

1491 *ot*] ? for *to* 1493 *I*] ? for *they* *faste*] *ste* altered from *rre* *make*] ? for *make one*
1494–1680 Hand C 1495 *2*] altered from *3* 1498 *why?*] *?* may be very low comma to follow *Rustcano* in 1497: it falls below *g* of *good* *it*] ? for *it is* 1501 *doost*] *t* vestigial 1503 *,(noe*] *(* obscures *,* 1505 *sownd*] *s* altered from *g*
1512 *lickour*] *c* retraced or altered 1518 *soakes*] *k*, ? blotted or altered

And still he roares &c.
yor [bro]drunkards a pure brother [FOL. 25a]
he hath our churches fashion
he nere did good deed he loues at his need
the spirits sweet copulation
And still he roares &c.
yor drunkard[s] is a miser
& an vsurer tis to be wondered
his cloaths are bare, he taks pots for his share
for free Gifts. xen in the hundred
And still he roares &c.
yor drunkard is a souldior
hele swagger, sweare & fight to
heele brag. heele, lye, heele cog ady
& steale like an ale howse knight to
And still he roares &c.
yor drunkard is a scoller
if beere once enters his pate sr..
his latine, his french, his logicke, his wench
are the things of the wch he will prate sir
And still he roares &c.
yor drunkard is a tradesman
the alehowse is his shop sir
he never thriues if once he wiues
because of the barley & hops syr
And still he roares &c.
Wherefore wee will be drunkards
because weele followe the fashion.
a good fellowe still, his Cuppe will fill
& drinke all like the dutch nation
And still wee[r] roare for some ale, for some liquor
O for some rich Tobacco.
we Raue, & sing and heavens vaults ring
as long as of beere theres no lacke ho../

1 say: Gram*er*y honest Rusticano, thou doest make a good apology for thy late intoxicated humor, & doest well excuse thy late ou*er*sight./

Rust: Doe I soe indeed. then blame me not for that heereafter, wch I can giue a [FOL. 25b] lawfull reason of, good fellowships: good fellowships Ile stand to it come lets in, lets in, Exeunt,

Enter Cælia the fayrie Queene in her night attyre

1539 *to*] *t* altered from long *s* 1549 *barley*] *ey* amalgamated 1550 *still*] *ti* smudged 1562 [1]*good*] *od* amalgamated [2]*good*] [2]*o* altered from *d*

Cæ: Murders. blacke mother, rapines midwife
Lusts infernall temptresse, guyde to fowlest sinne
fountaine of all enormous actions. night
horrid: infernall, derne, & ominous night
Run not, o Run not wth thy swarfy steeds
To fast a course: but driue light farre from henc^{e}
what ist[s] that hates the light but blacke offence
and I abhorre it, goying now to tempt
chastest Hyppolitus to hell bread lust
To thoughts most impious actions most vniust
bright Cynthia thou doest maske thy watry face
blushing to viewe me lust-polluted Queene
thy handmaides glittering starres doe rowle themselves
invelopt in some fog or vaporous cloud.
& blushing at my thoughts themselves thus shrowd
yet I must one, thus gods & men wth stood
my minds one fire, lusts heate inflames my bloud
faire Cytherea neu*er* could thou proue
such easeles heate, when thou didst Adon love
Dido thy thoughts were neu*er* soe inflamed
vpon Anchises sonne Æneas named
Torquine thy lust was great, compared to mine
but small: yet of the rest we neerest Combyne
what Can I say: my thoughts, my soule, my mind
doe yeeld to will, & reasons powers [but] blind.——shee goes to ye Red & awaks him,
how fares my knight

Red: Tell me what art thou called:
weele shewe thee what it is thus to disturbe vs——he pulls his sword from the boulst⟨er⟩,

[FOL. 26a]

Cæ: My lord awake yor spirits tis a woman
(that prickt wth kindnes/ comes to see & feele
yor sweetest welcome not relenteless steele
tis Cælia,

Red: fayrest fayrie Queene forgiue
my sleepefull aunsweare twas, (o doe beleeue
in troth [it] twas. in my not well wakened mind^{e}

Cæ: In faith ile credit thee then proue now kinde
I knowe thy spirits now are raised from sleep^{e}

Red: They are faire madame,

1572 *goying*] *oy* amalgamated: ? for *going*, or *joying* 1575 *watry*] *r* altered from *y* 1577 *handmaides*] ^{1}*a* altered from *n* 1583 *Adon*] *n* altered, ? from , 1587 *Combyne*] *ne* added 1590 *fares*] *e* altered or blotted 1595 *comes*] *c* altered, ? from *f* or long *s* 1596 *relenteless*] ^{3}*e* and ^{1}*s* added 1599 *(o*] *(* retraced 1600 *twas*] *t* added after deletion of *it*

Cæ: O then let me creepe
vnto thine armes, come, come, yo^{u} dreame not now.
Red: To this [bend] bright heauen shall bend before I bow
I knowe not whether senceles sleepe hath bounde
my sences still, or ame I in a sound^{e}
I knowe tis one of eyther Cælias chast
pure & harmeles, but thou (lewd & wast.
comest in her name, or some enchantique spell
thus to delude, me wch I know not well
Cæ: In faith tis Cælia that doth thus attend
at thy behest. o giue my sor⟨r⟩owes end
I ame a Queene, grant my request in this
Red: What ist[s] bright lady:
Cæ: nothing but a kisse
Red: If that be all then take it. He kisseth her:
Cæ: Troth I sweare;
Ile neu*er* dy indebted thus Ile Cleare
my self of all odde reckonings: whats behind;——shee kisseth him
Taste afore hand. if ought heere please yor mind^{e}
Red: O yo^{u} are to lasciuious: Phryna like
youle enter in my bed
Cæ: will yo^{u} not strike, [if]
if I offend yo^{u} fayth yor weapons dull
or yo^{u} a Coward, Chuse yo^{u} wch: o foole
Thou woest Hyppolitus whose thoughts are mild
intacted Chast: but thine, thine are defiled
They must haue vent, or natures frame will breake [Fol. 26b]
Canst loue me knight Come I prethee speake
Thy thigh me thinkes [.i]is soft, thy lips are red^{e}.
and soe are mine, let them enioyed one bed^{e}.
I needs must enter
Red: If yo^{u} enter heere
Like chast Xenocrates. ile Chast appeare
wthout all mocōn
Cæ: Ile like Phryna then
sweare tis a blocke I lye wth not a man
Red: Adventure if yo^{u} dare
Cæ: now by this kisse.
Ile hazard should I loose bright heavens blisse

1606 *bright*] interlined above deletion 1616 *What*] *W* altered from *To* 1622 *Taste*] *st* uncertain, ? *kt*; *t* altered from long *s* 1626 *I*] altered from false start 1632 *[.i] is*] altered, ? from *me* 1634 *enter*] ²*e* vestigial

Red: The effect doth followe, where the cause is first
and if it doe not nowe ile be accurst
The cause [is] was kissing: what the effect shall be
leap in the bed & you fayre Queene shall see
Cæ: I ame vnready yet most ready to: shee leps into ye bed:
Red: fye: we haue spoke to much let something doe
Cæ: I ame vndone, yet nothing haue we done
Red: I trust we shall by rising of the sunne
Cæ: knights tongues are swift theyr weapons very slowe
Red: you lye to open, gard yor self belowe
Cæ: I little feare yor forces:
Red: wth my dart
Ile pearce yor target framed [wth] by finest art
Cæ: but drawe the curtaines: for should [here] those heere see
our simple skill ashamed we should bee

Enter Rusticano

Heeres a coyle wth all my hart, I ame an arrant Rogue, but all the british knights (except my self/, are close in bed wth the ladyes: heere two men and one lady heere 3 men: 12 lasses: heere one & one by eache, in so much that theyr beds make more noise, then any foure creeking wheeles, of any dunkart in Lincolne: they exclude me for a wrangler: I can get noe Roome amongst them

I warrant you we [th]shall haue many lusty british ladds got to night, o what [FOL. 27a]
braue spirits haue those wenches, Ile warrant you one of them will tyre 4 of our best knights: hay, ho, I wonder what [kim] kyn this Rascally sleepe is to hunger, I Canot beleeue but tis his sonne, [it〈.〉] it makes a man gape & yawne soe, but see, I haue talked soe long, tis fayre day all abroad, and Goffer Phæbus is mounting his cart to goe to his worke, byre lady hee is a very early husband, nay there is never a whistling Carter in oxford shire shall driue soe farre in a whole day as he will doe in ane howre, for his horses [doe] as farre surpasse theirs: as butter milke doth whay: or chalke cheese: well by this tyme some be quite tyred: and Ile goe creepe [in som] into some warme place, it will neu*er* grieue an hungry man to cloy his appetite, to take an other mans leavings: Ieiunus stomachus raro vulgaria temnit: & by my fayth, I haue stomake, to any of the ladyes, but suppose that all the knights should be tyred wth theyr long iourneys, the wenches should all set upon me: sfut then I were cleane vndone, howsoever Ile venture for faint heart never vsed fayre lady/ Exit /

1644 *ile*] *l* altered, ? from *e* 1645 *was*] interlined above deletion 1654 *wth*] smudge over *t* 1655 *by*] interlined above deletion 1657 *simple*] *le* altered 1660 *heere*] *er*, ? amalgamated 1661 *by*] *y* altered from *e* 1663 *amongst*] *mo* blotted or altered 1665 *night*] *g* altered 1667 *sleepe*] followed by smudge in different ink 1671 *very*] *r* altered from *y* 1673 *as*] interlined above deletion with caret 1678 *tyred*] *r* altered or blotted *iourneys*] *ne* altered

Enter time
fortune yo^{w} see (Spectators guide the steps
of this her darelinge shilde the Red rose knight
yow see what favour the faerian dames
yelded to him & all his Company
whoe did abhorre all mens society
yet see meer straungers wuld soe much p^{r}vayle,
there woemanish fury force & strength[t] to quaile
& now imagine havinge stayed long space
wthin this frutefull soyle, [to thinke vpon] his thoughts are m⟨o⟩ovde
to thinke vpon his Sire whome he loved
when p^{r}sently (he comes wth full intent
thence to dep*ar*te) vnto his blest Content
sweet & delightfull Cælia (whoe soe grievd
to heare his resolu$\overline{con}$ as poore heart
Didoe was nere soe loath to let dep*ar*te
her stout Æneas). as she discontente
at his dep*ar*ture yet she did Consent
vpon his p*ro*mise gainde to make returne
heare yow may see how deeply she doth mourne
A Dumbe shewe [FOL. 27b]

Enter Red: & his followers, to them the fayry queen, & her Ladyes, they two whisp*er*, she weeps, at length he kisseth her and with great griefe they dep*ar*te, the like doe his followers & the ladies and exeunt, they beinge gone Cælia sownds the Ladies recou*er* her

The Redrose knight dep*ar*tinge as yo^{w} sawe
wth teare swolne eyes, tooke ship & hoyst vp sayles
but Cælias griefe was such as vanquisht sence
and all his power not of force to stand
in opposition to griefes dreadfull band
but yet by care, her sences were revievd
yet still shee grievd as of her ioy deprivde
the Red rose knight of whome I now must tell
how he obtainde his wish & what befell
him in the famowse Court of prester Iohn
within whose Corts yor thoughts must now suppose him
I trust yo^{w} will sit pleasde, my reasons this

1681–1855 Hand A 1681 *time*] *i* formed as *j*, with two dots 1684 *faerian*] *er* altered from *re* *dames*] *s* added 1686 *did*] *i* added 1688 *strength[t]*] ^{2}t added when ^{3}t was deleted 1690 *his . . . are*] interlined above deletion 1691 *loved*] *ed* amalgamated 1696 *Didoe*] *D* ? begun as *d* 1700 *deeply*] ^{2}e ? altered from *a* 1704 *departe*] *t* retraced or altered 1708 *eyes*] *s* added 1710 *all*] *a* altered, ? from *l* *of*] *o* altered, ? from *f* or *t* 1712 *revievd*] ^{2}e uncertain 1714 *Red*] *R* altered from *r* 1715 *obtainde*] *nd* smudged

They that nere loose time, can neu*er* doe amisse
Exit time

Enter Præster Iohn 2 lords before him & 2 after him with swords drawne, after them the Red and his followers

P I: Welcome renowned knights of Arthures Court
(one of the worthies of these happy tynes
fames trumpe hath soe [e]imbl⟨ec⟩onde forth the prays
of that thrise worthy monarch & his peers
as wee esteeme most blest our adged years
to live vntill this time in wich we see
knights of his table full of Chivalry
Welcome thrise welcome

Red thanks great Præster Iohn
thy clemency wee see to travellors
especially to Brittish shewes thy mynde
is truly noble affable and kinde
wee now are farre from Brittayne & our shipps
voyd of provision weather beaten ly
at Anchor in thy haven succoure then
our men & shipps if thou lovest Brittish men

P that gracious god wich we like yow adore
(if yow want succour) neu*er* aid me more
Commaunde what ere ye need

Om̄es thanks mighty lord [Fol. 28a]
th[e]y love weel second wth both heart & sword

P Yet tell me knights doth any knowe thats heare
the Red rose knight whose power hath noe peer
his fame hath ofte redownded in our Court
O honowre sownds each where his good report

Gal: Great Monarch here he is, whose warlike hand
neu*er* as yet could any knight wthstand

P is this the man

Red I am great potentate
recall the worthlesse prayse y[w]o spake of late

P first shall great Iove recall the day thats past
first shall the center in this Circle earth
be turnde to nothinge as yt was at firste
O heavens are y[w]o soe p*ro*pitious
vnto my silver hayres, as let mee see

1722 *followers*] *s* added 1724 *tynes*] *y* altered, ? from *r*; *n* for *m* 1725 *[e]imbl⟨ec⟩onde*] [1]*e* probably deleted 1735 *Brittayne*] *B* altered from *b* 1736 *provision*] *p* altered 1738 *Brittish*] *ish* altered, ? from *ys* 1742 *Om̄es*] *m̄* has four minims 1746 *his*] *s* retraced or altered

what I most wisht for this fælicity
Ru: Nay I am one of the company as well as the rest, if yow have heard
tidings of his p*ro*wesse yow must needs heare of myne, for he
& I haue bene in one an others company, this many a day
P If thart good friend weel affoord thee the better welcome
Ru: O lord sir I thanke yow wthall my heart, if I chaunce to
see yow yn kinge Karters Court, Ile requite yor kyndenes
La: Let not yor highnes be offended at him
hees but our Captaines iester or his foole
Ru: How yor captaines foole, yow are yor captaines asse, thers nere a pulake
in the world shall gieve me such words, let me come to him, yor captains
foole: Ile make him eat his words: O that a knight showld be so abusd
by ⟨a⟩——— I will not put yt vp thats flatte: yor captaines foole?
Red: peace sirha what mean yow
P Come hees miery man
now by our Crowne we can not but affecte him
yet tell vs knights what is the end yow aime
In this yor iowrney, at nought ells but fame
Red Truely great prince that was a motive to vs
our mynds are thirstinge after brave attempts
Strivinge to mount them selves above the sky [FOL. 28b]
for haughty feats of armes and Chivalry
yet theres an other ende, wch my attempts
wowld fayne attayne, for neu*er* Cowlde I tell
my lynage or descent, O easles hell
Mess: The queene and princesse, mighty liege attend
here for to see those englishmen, and pray
yow will admitte them
P willingly
Mess: make way roome for the queen & princesse
Red Mighty liege
Cannot yor queen app*ro*ach but[o] shee must crave
first licens of yor grace
P yea she must crave.
humbly & with submission: Loe they Come
Enter Q & princesse
Qu Helth to yor highnes
Ang: ioy vnto yor grace
P welcome sweete Bellamy, welcome guirle
doe honowre & gieve entertaine to those.

1762 *good*] ? for *his good* 1763 *lord*] *lo* altered from *w* 1764 *yn*] *y* altered from *I* 1766 *or*] *r* altered from *f* 1770 *foole*] *l* ? altered from *e* 1772 *miery*] *m* ? altered from *n* 1782 *easles*] [1]*e*, [2]*s* altered 1789 *but[o]*] *bu* altered from *vn* 1792 *submission*] *ub* retraced or altered

great Brittaines Champions and black envies foes
Q.Bell: Our hand we yeld yow to congratulat
yor former welcome
Om: thanks beloved queene
P Anglittora sweet wench, thy entertayne
ought be more lowly in an other vayne
Om: yor hande fayre Lady
P Come her mellow years
ara apte to kisse to her she neu*er* fears
Ru: Ile make clean my mowth, for if eu*er*y one have a smacke
at her, Ile make one thats flatt, I would they would
begin once, my mowth waters vengeausly at her
An Deare knight thy feature soe delights myne eys Asyde
that harte & hande & all thow dost surprise | they kisse her
Om yor mats Comaunde we thus fulfull
and Ile be one or ells ile misse my will Ru: kisseth her
Ang: how nowe ye base pesant
Ru: ifaith I am noe pheysant, but if I were, yt showld be on this Condition
that I showld be the Cocke & yow the hen, & then wee should well agree together
Red: Oh whither art transported,: oh my thoughts: Asyde [FOL. 29a]
till nowe ye neu*er* knewe what trulove meant
was yt some mellow downe, what lips? what paps?
where cupid sits invitinge passengers
I breathde my sovle (when that our lips did Ioyne)
into her breast, & there me thoughts inshrind
her eyes like to the Adamant constraynd
my sowle to lodge wth hers, Love, torment, payne
Ang: Howe sweetly did he clappe my palme in his Asyde
how fervently he gripte yt: peace he spies
the great imodesty of these fonde eyes
Red: The glaunces that she casts they wowld Captive
the purest mortall that remaynes alive
Ile Answer them in Language like her owne
although I Conquer I am ou*er* throwne
Ang: How greedily he looks: and still on me
hees caught I know, O blest congruity
Pre: frolicke brave knights, Come, come, lets in to feast
you shall have ntertaynmente of the best
Om: Weel follow: A hoars sownd wthin

1800 *beloved*] *d* altered 1802 *ought*] *ou* altered from *be* 1805 *kisse*] *is* altered from *ni* 1806 *clean*] *a* smudged 1807 *at*] *t* altered 1808 *once*] *nc* altered, ? from *w* 1809 *delights*] *d* altered, ? from *f* 1810 *harte*] *r* altered from *t* 1822 *like*] *l* altered from *k* 1824 *palme*] *a* altered 1828 *purest*] *u* resembles *a* 1832 *O*] altered, ? from *o* 1835 *hoars*] *a* resembles *o*

Red softe: whence is that dismall roare
fore heaven neu*er* was I yet soe scarde
tis some infernall monster: Cerberus
did neu*er* howle soe at the Thebans stroaks
Pr: This strikes our heart wth horrowe & amazemt
hearke and Ile tell ye, distant hence a mile
an horrid monster makes his dearne aboad
a fiery dragon treple tonged, huge,
deformed, fearfull, vast, and terrible
his belly like a tunne more h[e]arde then brasse
impenetrable clawes like serpents teeth
his tayle surpasseth iijee Cloth ells in length
In that Consists the greatest of his strength
sulpherous poyson (like to misty foggs
Comes from his hellish nostrills wich infecte
wth noysome sent the Confines of the ayre
were yt not for him wee showld surpasse in wealth
The Indian Monarch for he keeps a tree
of purest gowld, was once posest⟨e⟩ by mee
Red: Did neu*er* any mortall try his strength [Fol. 29b]
P: Too many worthy knights and all haue fell
by this fierce monster sent frō lowest hell.
Red: why, heres a coopemate for mee by the gods
nay by the brittaine borne
wch I esteeme more deare then dearest breath,
Ile coape this monster happen life or death,
P: Come come you shall not,
Red: By thy name great Arthur,
wch I esteeme most sacred, by my hopes
and by the St. I from my heart adore
Ile rouse thee fiend or neuer see thee more.
Q: Thy resolucon,s rash.
Red: Thus firme Ile stand
wth heart most strong, sword sure, and dauntles hand.
Brit: Had not our captaine spoken first, wee sweare
our lifes to hazardize to rid thy feare.
p: what generous spiritts beare braue bryttaines men

1841 *and*] *a* altered 1842 *his*] *h* altered from *d* 1843 *tonged*] *e* added *huge*] *u* altered from *o* 1847 *iijee*] [1]*i* altered from *t* 1848 *strength*] *r* altered from *h* 1849 *sulpherous*] [2]*u* has three minims *poyson*] *s* altered *to*] *t* followed by loop of an ascender

1856–71 Hand D 1866–8 in left margin, at right-angle to text, another hand, probably A, has tested his pen with the letters *Dy* or *By* 1871 *hazardize*] [1]*z* altered, ? from *t*

1872–9 Hand C

heere vs a little, why tis only fame
yor spiritts ayme at/ even a breath is gone
sooner then life fraile reputation

Red: O me twill [re]mount vs vppe
aboue the reach of dull obliuion
and wth high pitcht wings our name to all,
succeeding ages sings.
where is this fury.

P: Daughter all this while
you haue not vsed yor much p*er*swasiue stile
set on him wench.

Red: helpe mee sweete Cupid now (Aside.
A woman conquers mee if euer I bow

Ang: with bashfull modestie a virgin sues
to thee most haughty champion, o forbeare
to cast away thy life to all most deare
yet more then dearest vnto wretched mee (Aside
earths paragon for magnanimity⟨.⟩

Red: Madam impose yor knight the greatest taske [Fol. 30a]
yor heart can thinke of, were it like Hercules
to pash the boare wch thousands could not quell.
or force blacke fiends dance anticke-like through hell.
were it to conquer Alexander [great] like
all the vast territories of the world.
were it to coape the Olympicke thunderer
soe that myne honor I could harmles saue
I would effect all, or els dig my graue.
oh tis against mine honor what I vow
not to atcheeue but yet com̄aund mee now
faire princes to desist, Ile doe't wth shame
and blackest obloquie vnto my name.

Ang: His words like to some Necromanticke spells
haue charmed my tonge with silence, and my heart
In his firme passion seemes to act a part
⟨I no⟩ thing can withhold him gracious lord

Red: Our reputations credit is our word.

P: well sith it needes must bee Aurora's light
Shall bring thee thither magnanimious knight.

1880–1927 Hand D 1900 *what*] *w* altered or retraced *vow*] *w* altered, ? from *u* 1905 *silence*] 2*e* misformed 1908 *Our*] apparent comma after word is dot of *i* in *sith*, 1909 1909 *light*] apparent comma after word is dot of *i* in *knight*, 1910 1910 *magnanimious*] *s* altered, ? from *d*

meane while weele feast thee as our court affords.
come let vs in to sport attend vs lords. Ex. manet Ang.

Ang: Since gallant knight my praiers cannot mooue thee
my death shall show it if thou diest I loue thee. Ex.

Rusticano pulles S^{r}. Lancelot backe

Rust. A word with yo^{u} Sr Lance lout.

Lan: what dost thou call mee Lancelout.

Rust. is not yor name so?

Lanc: Thou knowst my name I am sure tis Lancelot.

Rust. howsoeuer I am afraid it will fall to yor lot to bee the lout, but lea= uing this I pray you what doe yo^{u} call this fine lord that vseth vs soe kindly⟨,⟩,

Lan: His name is great Prester Iohn.

Rust: Great priest Sir̄ Iohn call yee him, hee is not soe great a priest as our sir Iohn a Lincolne neither hath his nose soe many rubies on, althoughe indeed hee hath more on's apparell, hee hath gay clothes indeed, but our m^{r} parson goes in a threed bare [clo] coate wth long skirts, a pen and an inkorne, hanging by his side, a payre of spectacles, hanging about his necke [FOL. 30b] very deuoutly: but as for this priest sr Iohn I promise you I neu*er* sawe th⟨e⟩ like,

Lanc^{e} Thou art mistaken man his name is the great prester Iohn the lord of this land & not priest sr Iohn as thou tearmest him.

Rust: well prester Iohn or priest sr Iohn alls one for that, I dare lay a wager wth yo^{u}, though he hath more gay Cloathes, then our m^{r} parson, yet he is n⟨ot⟩ an honester man

Lanc^{e} yor reason Rusticano

Rust: why ile tell yo^{u} my reason: hee is the quietest plainest fellowe in christendome wth his parishion*er*s, heele neu*er* goe to lawe wth them as many of yor rangling fellowes will doe, about tyethes or fat pigges or the Ale, nay Ile be sworne I haue knowen a priest goe to lawe wth his parishion*er*s for the least things they had, as eggs & chicknes, & piggeons, nay even of very cruds he must haue a bowle sent him, but as I tould yo^{u} or m^{r} parson is an other gest fellowe, heele drinke 2 or 3 ciuill potts wth his neighbor vpon a sunday or holiday after eusom: he reeds an homily once a quarter he preacheth once a tweluemoneth: & then he will not like yor royling p*re*chors speake against our good meetings, our dancing on sundayes, our may-games, our som̄er poles & the like, nay heele praise, our neighbour-

1911 *thee*] interlined above caret 1912 ^{1}*vs*] *v* altered 1920 *yor*] *y* altered, ? from *l* 1923–4 additional space between lines 1926 *apparell*] ^{1}*l* altered
1928–92 Hand C 1937 *plainest*] *n* has three minims 1939 *Ale*] *l* ? retraced or altered from *k* 1941 *eggs*] ^{1}*g* retraced or altered 1943 *fellowe*] *o* retraced or altered 1944 *eusom*] *m* with final descender may be meant for *ng*, ? for *euensong* 1946 ^{2}*our*] *u* retraced or altered *sundayes*] *a* altered or blotted

like feastings & meetings: and he himself will [goe⟨.⟩] Come & tast a Cuppe of my
lords ale, & eate a Cheasecake or twoe, & soe goes away very soberly
one time indeed [very] aboue the rest, he was very fiery, exclaiming against
the corruptions of the tyme, & that wherein he did particularize was
of the Childrens ill breeding wch did breake his glasse windowes & sr [re]
reuerenc^{e} against his walls, shroud matters I Can tell yo^{u} they would
move any mans patienc^{e} very much

Lanc^{e}. But after what man*er* did he leade his life

Rust He was very painefull & laborious, he would carry mucke into the field
in winter, he would make hey very well in sommer, nay Ile be sworne I
my self haue seene him ride in a wayne amongst a Company of litle
Children: wth a pikeforke one his necke hee is soe lowly: [but af]

Lance: Come come thou hast held me in a tale heere: while wee loose all the good
cheere wthin.

Rust: say yo^{u} so. I would yo^{u} had told me soe sooner, & then I had been briefer [FOL. 31a]
but howsoever it is better to Come to the later end of a feast then the
beginning of a fray: & therefore Ile leaue yo^{u} & run my way Ex:

Lanc^{e}. Well ile followe yo^{u} for this onc^{e}.
Stout Tom a Lincolne whatsoere befall
thy dauntles forc^{e} the like will suffer all Exit./

Enter Cælia. her hayre hanging carelesly wth her babe
[hanging care] in her armes, & 2 ladyes &c^{c}.

1 Lady Right gracious Queene returne againe to Cort
abide not thus vpon this stony Rocke
both day & night expecting his returne
whoe nougte respects yo^{u} whilest yo^{u} thus doe mourne o

2 la: o let [vs] not vs depriued be of yor sight
wch is our blisse, our solac^{e} & delight

Cæ: Alas. yo^{u} Canot feele the griefe I doe
yo^{u} little knowe what panges: what tortures throbs
Dolours, vexa$\overline{cons}$: strike my fainting breast
for losse of him: was natures rarest Iewell
and yet to me, (poore me/ he proues most cruell
wherefore Ile neu*er*, neu*er* make returne
but one this Rocke Ile lye, and ever mourne

1 La: sweet princes if yor resolution's such
yet [su] Cease yor teares, wipe dry yor blubbered eyes
o breake not furth into those shrikes & cryes

1951 *corruptions*] ^{2}*o* retraced or altered 1955 *maner*] *er* suspension formed as *d* 1956 *carry*] ^{2}*r* added or altered 1958 *amongst*] *o* altered or blotted 1959 *hee*] *h* altered from *v* or *w* 1962 ^{1}*had*] *ad* amalgamated *briefer*] *i* altered from *e* 1965 *ile*] *e* altered from *l* 1967 *suffer*] *ff* altered or blotted 1968 *carelesly*] *ly* altered, ? from *h* 1969 *2*] altered from *3* 1973 *mourne*] *o* altered 1974 *yor*] *yo* altered from *ou* 1977 ^{1}*what*] mark over *w* suggests false start 1984 *dry*] *y* altered

2 La: Doubtles hee will returne: if not you haue
his perfect picture in yor armes & hart
This lad must needes extenuate yor smart
he seemes soe like his father o Content
yor self wth sight of him, cease to lament
Cæ: Bid Phæbus cease to shine, bid fiercest tygres
Cease to be sauage,: bid stout lyons cease
to roare when hunger gnawes them bid the wolfe [FOL. 31b]
cease to be ravenowes, bid Lawyers Cease
to take theyre fees, bid all men live[inge] in pease
rather then bid me sorrowes Clowds dy'pell
by pleasures sunshine o yow then doe well
2 La: Madam if griefe will Cause him backe repayre
well [yow] might yow greave then,
Cæ O yow are made of stone, [th]
that Can not weepe & grieve & Cry & moane
but heare me ladyes let ther eu*er* burne
great fire vpon this high & steep downe Cliffe
that if mild neptune steere his Course this way
yt may invite him hither ladies see
what wee Cōmaund furthwth effected bee
1 La: we goe great princess heaven graunt yow ease
& may yor sighs & sobs & sorrows sease Exe: La:
Cæ O would this rock were framde of Diamond
(then like a load stone would yt force his ships
if ere the windes did drive him hither wards
to anker here where I expecte him thus
& were he once enfowlded in these armes
not life nor death not all the world showld gaine him
my rose my knight whose absens is my payne
what did I wish I had him in these armes
see here a model of him, p̄rty infant
why smiles my boy theres rather cause of grief
thy dad hath lefte vs childe, troth he smiles still
alasse thy mynd & thoughts are voyde of ill
the Ladies are returnde
La: Right wofull queene
the fires wee have made full farre are seen

1991 *shine*] *h* altered from *t* or *l* *tygres*] *es* amalgamated
1993–2078 Hand A 1995 *live[inge]*] [1]*e* altered from *in*, *ge* deleted *in*] interlined above caret *pease*] *p* altered, ? from *C*
1996 *dy'pell*] *y* altered, ? from *p* 2008 *Exe :*] *e* altered from *:* , *:* added 2017 *model*] *d* altered 2018 *grief*] *i* altered from *e* 2019 *lefte*] *l* altered from *v* *troth*] *r* altered from *h*

Cæ thanks ladies thanks our Child we here Comit
vnto yor tender care each day lets see yt
twill eas vs somewhat, hence griefs at eas
when tis most solitary, then twil cease
leave vs we pray
La This our hopes shalbe
Heaven at length will ease y$\overset{r}{\bar{o}}$ misery

Exeunt: Cæ: at one dore, La: at another

Enter Red: Gall: L: T: Rus: [FOL. 32a]

Red [g] Goodmorrow friends the Chearfull lark hath rowsde
and wakte vs from our slumber see the morne
is newly risen & Auroras blush
doth tell vs that her lover now begins
for to amount his great Eburnean Carre
And one the mountayne tops he red app*er*s
the Corts not vp Come exclude all fears
wee must goe cope the Dragon
Gall this earth shall passe away
before Ile leave or sturre from thee this day
L if La: now his friends for sake o then
nere wer I⟨e⟩ worthy for to live mongst men
T shall Tr: budge one foot, noe showldst thow dy
wich heaven defend weel follow in stantly
Red Away yo^{v} should not
Om: truely but we will
we loved thee eu*er* and we love thee still
Red well since yo^{v} will Celestiall spirits save
our mountinge sowles earth is o[r]^{r} bodies grave
fare well good rusticano back[⟨r⟩] returne
if this attempt doe slay vs neu*er* mourne
Great Præster Iohn I know will tender thee
and for our sakes affecte thee hartily

Ru O lord I could euen weep out my heart at this discourtesy offered me (fare
well good Rus:) would any man in the world thinke I would bid thee
farewell wch have followed thee throughout all Countereys as I have
done, whoe left his sheepe in Lincolne to follow thee, Rust: whoe
left his fine minikin iug to follow thee, Rusticano who wente
wth thee from barnesedale heath to kinge Karters Cort, Ru: whoe

2026 *vs*] interlined 2028 *pray*] ? for *pray you* 2034 *vs*] *v* altered from long *s* 2040 *Dragon*] *D* altered from *C* 2044 *wer*] *w* altered from start of *I* 2045 *Tr :*] oblique stroke over *:* may indicate contraction 2048 *but*] *bu* altered from *we* *will*] *i* altered or blotted 2051 *mountinge*] *un* has three minims *o[r]^{r}*] ^{r} added above deletion *bodies*] *i* formed by dotting first stroke of *e* 2053 *this*] *t* altered, ? from *v*; *is* added *attempt*] *a* altered 2055 *sakes*] ^{2}*s* altered or retraced 2056 *Ru*] altered from *L :* *euen*] ^{2}*e* altered from *er* suspension 2058 *Countereys*] ^{1}*e* uncertain

went into ffraunce wth thee Ru: who fought there when he Could not choose, Ru: who returnde home wth a more willing mynd then eu*er* he went, Ru: whoe travelde ou*er* all the world wth thee Rust: whoe (exempli gratia went with thee to spayne, Ru: who went with thee into Italy, Ru: who went wth the into Asia, Affrica Europ, Holland, Polland, denmark, Swethland, O that I could number them, whoe went into eu*er*y place wth thee, Ru: whoe came to the queene of fayries wth thee, Ru: whoe was drunke there for company with thee, Ru: whoe mischieft & metagrabolizde fower ladyes Collosodiums in one night: Ru: who [FOL. 32b] came now to priest sir Iohns Court wth thee, and whoe will goe wth thee in spight of all gaynsay yt, Rusticano returne quotha I could ene spoyle this goodly Countenance wth weping at yor vnkindenes:

Red: Come we have stayed to longe, yo^w saving powers
hover, o hover wth yor wings of safety
this day & eu*er* ou*er* our harmelesse heads
this monster heere is set men to destroy
o [doe,] let [y]our swords then roote him cleane away

Om: Thy orizons are heard. heauen prosp*er* thee
And vs in this blacke infortunity./ ——Exeunt om̄nes

sown̄d. Enter P: Iohn. Queene/ Ang: lords & the rest./

P: did the⟨y⟩ soe secretly dep*ar*te away
none knowing but thy self

1. L: They did great Lord
when thus say they Comend vs to his grace
and if the Chance of fight proues ominous
vnto our (ever yet successfull acts
as that we p*er*ish by the monsters gripes
yet let his grace soe thinke those knights are dead.
whome for his sake not all the world should dread

P: Prosp*er* o prosp*er* them celestiall graces
and let them proue as happy as heroike
protect them from the piercing dragons sting
then hymnes & psalmes wee in theire praise will sing

Q: Inough my lord noe doubt the powers diuine
will heare yor earnest prayer ioyned wth mine

Ang: And Can Ang be silent then

2063 *mynd*] *m* altered, ? from *y* 2068 *them*] *m* altered from *n* 2069 *fayries*] *y* altered, ? from *o*; *e* altered from *d* by added *s* 2071 *metagrabolizde*] *ra* (? *re*) altered from *ro* *Collosodiums*] 3*o* perhaps *e*

2079–2170 Hand C 2079 *set*] *e* blotted 2082 *om̄nes*] *mn* has four minims 2083 *sown̄d*] *nd* altered *lords*] *l* altered from *&* 2084 *the⟨y⟩*] *y* unformed, but implied by size of flourish after *e* 2089 *our*] *u* unformed, ? for *or*

o noe giue eare protector of all men
thou doest respect the heart, o then view mine
saue helpe and succour at this helples tyme
if eu*er* thou hadst pitty o then saue
my lord, my husband from a timeles graue.

Enter Rust. amazedly Running & looking one the king.

p: I: Speake Rust: kill my heart wth griefe [Fol. 33a]
I knowe the rose of Brittaines withered
and one them all this Hidra now is fed

Ang: Heigh ho. ye heauens take my soule hees gone
whose all it was. & onelie his alone.——shee sounds

p: Looke to the princes

q: Speake Anglitera
it is thy mother that intreats thee speake
sweet daughter drawe thy sences backe againe——shee recou*er*s
s[h]ee, shee recou*er*s ou*er*prest wth paine

Ang. despightfull fortune couldst thou be soe crosse
or why :(if needs thou must be ominous
wouldst thou not tell me: [i]that I might haue died
wth natures paragon & valours pride.
thou squint-eyed minion (ile /wingd wth revenge/
beg leaue [wh⟨o⟩] of Ioue, to mount beyond the starrs
venus & thee Ile hale from yor bright carres
for [he] shee & thee[e] eye both in one Conspire
to robbe me of the Iewell I desyre
weare you enamored of him? yes tis soe
fury and hell bread fiends. they laugh & toy
& dandle him, to make their sport & ploy
what can you suffer this supreamest powers
looke how they point at me. & laugh & smile
& Can I then be patient all this while./
ye powers of horrour you I invocate
aide & reveng me/ what is it to late
whose helpe shall I implore patience guide
the serne of Reason for I nowe Run wide.

p: what sudden passion's this: send seeke for helpe
where or whoe ever: Bellamy like care
ti[i]s ill wth vs. if that shee evill fare./

2105 *amazedly*] *m* altered 2115 *s[h]ee*] *h* heavily retraced and blotted 2117 *thou*] *th* altered from *y* 2118 *[i]that*] 1*t* altered from *f* *might*] *g* altered from *h* 2120 (*ile*] (written over : *wingd*] *g* altered or blotted 2121 *of*] interlined above deletion 2122 *bright*] *g* altered 2123 *shee*] *s* altered from *t* *eye*] ? for *aye* 2135 *passion's*] *n* altered; original ascender of following letter altered to ' *this*] *t* formed over *of* 2137 *ti[i]s*] written as *his*, then altered to *tis* by deletion of *i*

Q: In what we may wee will our form*er* [iy] ioy [FOL. 33b]
is turned to sorrowe griefe and great annoy—— Exit Q: & her la: wth ye prince./
P Speake man that all this w[⟨t⟩]hile amazed stands
what hath befallen our champions
Rust: Amazed: say ye: I ihinke I had good cause to bee amazed, yet would
haue skarred. the stowtest he that is present out of his witts
[a]for doe ye see sir, wee were noe sooner out of the cityes viewe &
alltogeathe serious in talke of the successe of the battell, but we
heard such a roare, as if heaven and earth would haue come
togeather, now sr I began to Runne very slowly: not to see wch way
the Roare Came, but very fairely away, as fast as ever my legs
could Carry me, but that Sr Lance: a vengeanc^{e} take him, he is
ever my enemy: Caught fast hould on my arme, and very dis-
courteously would not let me goe, well we went forward alittle
further, but we hard such an other yell as if all the bulls in y⟨e⟩
world had beene togeather they could not make such a noise, when I
hard it by the force of my arme I put valour to flight: I meane
I broke from sr lanc: [f⟨.⟩ll] in spite of his teeth. & then all the rest
did sett vpon me & forct me to stay, & soe at length to make a shart tale
of it, wee Came to the goulden tree, but I had scarce had my viewe of
it/ but there ariseth one a suddaine out of a darke Caue, a lord me
thinkes hee is still at my heeles, there Comes me out I say this wild dragon
whoe when he stood vpon his feet was as bigge as a mountaine, &
when he sawe vs he bellowed furth such a hoarse sownd, as stroake most
valiant me vnto the ground, they say gold Can doe all things. yet if all
the trees in the world were all pure gold & mine if I should haue
stayed. Could not haue let me from Running away: nay I beate sir Lanc^{e}.
threwe downe sr Trist: tosst sr Gall: like a tenis ball, & the Red [rose]
had he not beene my m^{r} had dipt his finger in the same sauc^{e}, but for pitty
sake I spared him, & soe Came Running away in that furious amazement
yo^{u} sawe me/
[P:] I But were the knights slaine by the monsters fange
Rust: Nay that yo^{u} may goe aske them & youle knowe for me/
P: yet there is hope, o thou that canst do all [FOL. 34a]
preserve and saue those knights frō luckles fall. { A shout w^{t}hin
whence is that shout, (enter Messenger)
Messen: Renowned prester Iohn [⟨w⟩]

2138 *ioy*] *i* altered, ? from *n* 2142 *yet*] ? for *yt* (it) 2143 *skarred*] *k* altered from *t* 2146 *would*] *l* altered from *d* 2147 *Runne*] *nn* has three minims 2147,2150 *very*] *r* altered from *y* 2156 *shart*] *h* altered from *t* 2162 *valiant*] *n* has three minims, ? *un* 2167 *furious*] *u* has one minim but no dot 2168 *yo^{u}*] ^{u} altered, ? from ^{r}
2171–2243 Hand D 2172 *luckles*] *k* altered from *l*

wee stood vpon yor pallace battlements.
and many a thousand on their houses top
to view the combat wch the Red Rose knight
had wth the dragon.

p: Come declare the fight
The shoute foreshewes its good,

Mes: Then thus it was
The monster hauing spied the Red Rose knight
wth flaggy wings displaied bout flings his taile
roaring forth such a dismall yell or crie,
as if great heauens frame had crackt in sunder
wth great confusion, and the earth dissolued
and roring thus hee strikes his scaly tayle.
full at the head of him, who wth his sword
puents the stroake, and strikes his asunder
oh now who would haue seene true rage indeed
herein the abstract, might haue cast their eies
vpon the irefull direfull drāgons fumes.
wch came as from a furnace, belching out
such cries and sounds as stroke him in a sound.
I meane the Red Rose knight whom each man thought
his latest blow hee had most dearley bought
for now the dragon held him in his phangs.
griping and gnawing, tossing him halfdead.
at last hee puls the hellmet frō his head
and saued his life, hauing receaued fresh aire
but what good could it [doe] prooue thoughe hee reuiued
his danger now was greater then before
his flesh most greeuously hee rent and tore
yet neuer dying memory releeued
this gallant knight who thus long had beene greeued
for thinking on his dagger out he pulles[,] it,
& fast (thats in his clawes) Renowned King [FOL. 34b]
hee reeued it to the hilt ithe right side wing
wch place of all the rest was farre most weake
the monster feeling all his strength abated
seekes thence to flye aloft, the Red Rose knight
p*er*ceauing his intent wth dauntles force
soe plies his strokes (that fel as thicke as hayle)

2182 *Red*] *d* ? added 2186 *confusion*] *s* ? altered 2189 *his*] ? for *his tayle* 2199 *the*] *t* added 2200 *his*] *s* altered from *m* *life*] *f* altered, ? from *c* 2206 *he*] *e* altered from *it* *[,] it*] *it* added, obscuring ,

that hee the dragons fury soone doth quaile
and now life's vanisht when on bended knee
hee thanks the giuer of all victory.

p: O neuer heard of combat this doth grace
his king and countrey, blessed bee the tyme
that did conduct him to this now blest clime
for hee hath made vs happie messenger
thy newes hath solac't our late mornefull heart
for wch our bounty giues thee this reward
‘‘ good newes wth kind acceptance still are heard
(begon when please thee.

Mess.. Heauens blesse the king
O may I euer such like tydings bring.

P: wee wish thou mayst, lord how long they stay
meethinke it best to meete them on the way.

2 lo: You need not mighty prince for here they come

A flourish enter the people wth palmes in their hands crying the Red Rose Knight; hee himselfe after him all bloudy: bearing in one hand his sword wth the Dragons head on the points, in the other the sprig of gold his 3 followers.

Red: Health to thy maiestie I here present
my loue and seruice, first the dragons head
and in the same here stands the 3 fierce tongues
wch oft did vomite vp sulph⟨u⟩reous flames
here is a sprigge wch maugre all the forc^{e}
the now tam'd monster had I lopped of
from that bright tree of gold the monster kept
and here as due I render to yor grace
the spoiles I won onely my loue embrace.

p: Thankes worthy brittaine after tymes shal see
insculpt [thy] in brasse thy magnanimity./
thy self shall stand in marble pillar framed [FOL. 35a]
and these thy acts in order shalbe named
A stranger knight vpon our shore dyd land
and slewe a three tongued dragon by his hand
heere is the head and heere the golden tree
this to succeeding tymes this knowen shall be

Red: Cease mighty p: I: farre let there be
such thoughts remoued from yor maiesty

2218 *tyme*] *y* altered from *h* 2232 ^{2}*the*] *t* added: *e* altered from *is* *gold*] *l* altered from *o* 2236 *sulph⟨u⟩reous*] ^{2}*u* blotted, ? *o* 2237 *forc^{e}*] ^{e} added 2239 *from*] *m* added 2243 *in*] interlined above deletion with caret 2244–2317 Hand C 2245 *shalbe*] *b* altered from *l*, *e* added *named*] *d* added 2246 *stranger*] *t* altered

Enter Ang: runing wth her hayre about her eares
yo^{u} would needes let him goe like hard hearted men as yo^{u} were, alas
poore rose, doest weepe at theire vnkindnes, to thinke that they would send thee
(a stranger/ to be devoured of such a strang monster, thou mayest weepe well
enough, come dry thine eyes, dry thine eyes, I fayth thou art worth them
all, nay better then all of them: yet see the spite [of⟨.⟩it,] ont, hee's lost, hee's dead
not all the world Can recover him, nay where there thousand worlds they
were not of value to recall him, all to little, all to little, hee was more deare
to me then dearest life, o gods what had Ang. deserved that yo^{u} should
proue to me soe yrefull, as hauing in the world one only I held most pretious
that to take from me, would it not moue to spleene patienc^{e} it self, yo^{u}
Canot pitty: wherefore then doe I iust like to women⟨:⟩ weepe, whyne, & cry
noe patienc^{e} I scorne thee, thou art fit for none but fooles, [s⟨a⟩ys] bearials
such as women are, noe,

Ile drag. Tysyphone by her curled locks
And mount the Car of pale fac'd Hecate
pulling the fatall sisters from theyr wheele
ile wrest the neck of cruell Atropos
because shee broke the [fatall] vitall threed of's life
wch Clotho would traduce for many yeares

oh what a braue minded wench was the Carthaginian dydo, what a couragious
heart had shee, & is Æneas shipt & gone, come he⟨e⟩rt prepare thy self to
mone, (shee pulls forth her knife/ ile mone as shee did, grieue as shee did
lament as shee did: come pretty engine thou wilt soone transport me to fayre
Elizium, where my louer sits, crowned wth roses, & wth vernant bayes
dect wth all blisse, & wth eternall dayes.
dost Call me, lo: I come, but I pray thee entreate churlish Charon to giue me passage
freely soe, soe dost Call againe, I hast sweet Brittaine, I hast, good night to all
the world⟨,⟩ (shee stabbs at her self but misseth by falling/

p: Looke to my daughter there: o what disastre [FOL. 35b]
hath caused this mischiefe: see shee hath slaine her self
heere lyes the knife that dyd it, o tis true

Red: Not soe my lord the heavens are more mild
to faire Ang. yor princely Child
the knife hath mist her,

P: O eternall thankes

Red: And I the same retribute, (had shee dyed Aside
this life would soone haue followed: royall princes,

2258 *world*] *l* altered from *d* 2261 *only*] altered from *onee* by changing ^{2}*e* to *y*, leaving ^{1}*e* to be read as *l* 2269 *ile*] *e* altered from *l* 2270 *shee*] *s* begun as *h* *vitall*] interlined above deletion with caret 2272 *was*] interlined above caret 2273 *Æneas*] *Æ* altered, ? from *An* 2275 *transport*] *ort* badly formed 2276 *vernant*] *ve* amalgamated 2289 *princes,*] , altered from *:*

how ist, how fares yor grace
Ang: O very well
now I ame hither come wth me to dwell/ shee recoue*rs*
how sweet this place is
Red: O recall yor sences
see heeres yor father wth his Royal traine
whoe greatly feared that you had beene slaine./
Ang: Nere tell me soe man, o wilt thou delude me
twas for thy sake alone[s] I slewe my self
to meet thee heere in lou*er*s happines
and wilt thou now forsake me, canst thou be
soe farre ingratefull vnto loving me
before thou wast mild affable and kind
beare, o beare not now soe hard a mind
Red: Good madame thinke vpon yor pristine state
yor loue to me will Cause yor fathers hate——
the hell bred fury wth our stroakes is stownd
and weltring in his gore, dead one the grownd
recall yor self ————Shee recoue*rs*
Ang: O praised be yor power her [self]
P: for what deere daughter sencs.
Ang: for recou*er*y
of my lost sences father p*ar*don me
my frenzy did offend yor maiesty
p Pardon thee child for what, alas poore soule
I praise the sacred deity for this
in that I haue regaind my late lost blisse
goe Lord & tell the queene of this glad newes
meane while sweet princesse comfort to mine age [Fol. 36a]
ioy to my heart and pleasure to my soule
I heare comitte vnto thy skilfull hand
this haughty knight who by his hardines
hath slaine Chymœra to our great content
proue Æsculapius [to a] and recure his wounds.
whose name the land of P: I: shall sound.
Ang: Leaue it to mee my lord my skill shall shew
how soone Ile salue his sore, how ist braue knight
why is yor colour chang'd
Red⟨:⟩ Madam I bleed

2296 *slaine*] *l* altered, ? from *h* 2306 *stownd*] *o* altered or retraced 2309 *praised*] blot or deletion between *p* and *r*
2311 *recouery*] *co* altered, ? from *ad*; *y* retraced 2315 *deity*] *y* added
2318–91 Hand D

And 'gin to faint through too much losse of blood
my wound is deepe and doth require yor arte
tis deepe indeed I feele it at my heart asyde
Ang: Dread lord wee must entreate yor maiesty
a litle to forbeare the knight's not well.
P⟨:⟩ Perhaps his hardy trauell had this day
by night doth thus perplexe him weele away (Ex: P I and all his lord⟨s⟩,
Ang: How fare you sir Ile warrant you ne're feare manet Red Rose and Ang.)
Red: Lady my wound is dangerous I sweare.
my heart is pierc'd what hope can I expect
vnles yor grace alone doth mee protect
Ang: Tis but yor mind my lord Ile pawne my word
my selfe will salue it,
Red: you much ioy affoords
Ang: Lets know the depth of it
Red: Oh those starrelike eies
wch once decaied all earthly beauty dies
those blazing comets they haue made the wounds
and you haue pawned yor word to make mee sound
I claime yor promise come youle keepe yor word,
salue what you soared and pleasaunt healthe afford
Ang: [Ah] are you soe craftie 'faith Ile not recall
my vow once made take heart, take hand, take all.
All I com̄itte vnto thee I call mine
Red: I all and more then all I thus resigne (he kisseth her)
Sweete heauens rauish not my vitall spirits
wth surfet on this earthly paradise [Fol. 36b]
Anglitora when I proue false to thee
Ioue's tri-sulkt Thunder strike mee suddenly.
Ang: When I a Cressida to Troylus proue
let gods, men, diuells hate my faythles loue,
I would all maydens here would learne of mee
not to delay their louers constancie
not to denie what honest loue doth craue
but if yor minds concurre loue let them haue
" True loue's impatient of delay that's true
bee kind to men if men proue kind to you
Do not disdaine wth (I cannot loue)

2329 *faint*] *t* altered, ? from *e* 2331 *asyde*] forms of *s* and *y* suggest that SD may not be in Hand D 2336 *Ile*] *I* altered or retraced *manet . . . Ang.)*] between 2335–6 2341 *selfe*] *f* altered, ? from *u* 2343 *Lets*] *s* added 2349 *healthe*] *t* added 2351 [3]*take*] *t* resembles *k* 2355 *wth*] ? for *wch* 2360 *here*] interlined above caret 2365 [2]*kind*] *d* altered, ? from *e* 2366 *disdaine*] ? for *disdaine them*

the contrary yo^{u} know and men oft proue
if men affect yo^{u} and yo^{u} them the like
if freinds do not consent the match vp strike
yet first entreate them to consent thereto
see if they will, if not wed, bed, and [doe] wooe
ought man to sell his child as beasts are sold
oh loue is neuer priz'd wth coine or gold
by wealth or goods or substance oh not soe
their fault's the greater that soe vse to doe
Red Inowgh sweet princesse come let's now approue
how to combine our firme-vnited loue.
Ang: why, lets dep*ar*t whilst thus nocturnall silence
hath husht vp all in secret cynthias light
may safe conduct vs to yor ships this night.
Red: I see yo^{u} loue mee deare Anglitora
to follow mee a stranger and forsake
yor parents friends and countrey for my sake
yet first Ile see p*er*haps the king will giue
yor selfe as wife to mee
Ang: Not whilst wee liue.
Red: Haue not I freed him and his land from thrall
Ang: I know yo^{u} haue and made him rich wthall.
Red: How [he] can hee then denie mee?
Ang: Oh hee vow'd
first in the [y]earths vast busome to bee shrowd
before that hymen ever should conioyne [Fol. 37a]
in nuptiall knot a strangers hand and mine
but one of my alliaunc^{e} must me wed
and first descend into my virgin bed
This is his will
Red: But Ile thy bed ascend
thou louest & tenderst me thy dearest friend
Ang: Witnes bright heavens [h⟨.⟩]
Red: Ang: shall see,
how soone her wishes shall accomplisht be⟨:⟩
s^{r} lanc: Trist: & sr Gallowine
Rowse from yor slumbers, c⟨o⟩me lets hoise vppe sayles
the wind blowes mee⟨rily⟩ and nothing fayles
Arise I say

2370 *entreate*] ^{1}*t* added 2379 *secret*] *c* added *light*] *t* altered from *e* 2388 *made*] *d* altered
2392–2427 Hand C 2397 *ascend*] *d* altered from *t*, or clumsily completed 2399 *[h⟨.⟩]*] apparently false start for *how*, 2401
2403 *sayles*] *l* altered from *e*

Om: wee come for to attend
yor will and pleasure — Enter his followers as from theyr bedds

Red: Hast I pray you hast
& let our ships be in a redines
weele strike into the deepe & launch from shore
neu*er* to see this famous Iland more
make speed & back returne Ang: — Exeūt follo:
prepare whats needefull, for our swift dep*ar*ture
Ile bring thee to a[⟨.⟩]nation shall adore
and serue thee fitting to thy great estate
hast & away the night growes very late

Ang: I goe I, goe this is my comfort still
tis true loue forced me not my froward will — Exit

Enter Rusticano wth one hose of the other one, wthout any brichis

Rust: Hoyda, what a coyle & sturre is heere, what a poxe ayle you trowe, can
not a man sleepe in quiet for you. heere's⟨,⟩ a rising & running, & rowling
and Rumbeling, that a man canot take the least nap in the world, for yor
talking of ships and oares, and in a readines, and I Cañot tell what, I
thinke yor wits Run a wooll gathering. how now, what meanes this
one hose of, neu*er* a band, noe brichis, I would I might be flayed. if yor
bawling did not almost affright me out of my fiue sences, you may see
how I started vppe, nay my very tayle roared for feare when I rose./
I thought verily some howse had bene one fire & now I see [FOL. 37b]
they are one fire to be goinge: but I warrant yow the water
will soone Coole theyre heat, well Ile goe in and make
my selfe ready preparde, but yt shalbe for an other
nap — Exit

Red: Prowe gentle Trident Neptune, let thy Calme
be most auspicious to our happy voyage
o let thy billows smooth as Ise Conducte vs
let thy three forked mase steeere these our ships
wth safest waftage to our longe wisht haven
to Englande happy England wich I lefte
In hope to finde my father, but since fates
have thus ordainde yt I will bakce returne
to grace thy front wth all those victories
I have acheevd wth vallours hardines

2406 *wee*] *w* altered from *Y* 2407 *bedds*] 2*d* uncertain 2410 *weele*] 3*e* added 2411 *more*] otiose stroke over *m* 2412 *Exeūt*] *eu* retraced or altered 2413 *whats*] *s* added *swift*] *w* altered from *h* 2414 deleted letter may be *n* 2417 *I goe I,*] 2*I* added after writing of *goe* 2418 *froward*] *o* altered 2419 *brichis*] 2*i* doubtful 2420 *&*] retraced 2421 *for*] second stroke added to *r* 2425 *if*] loop above *i* like false start of *f*
2428–2532 Hand A 2432 *Exit*] *x* altered from *n* 2436 *three*] *r* altered from *e*, *ee* added *ships*] *h* altered from *p* 2440 *returne*] *r* altered, ? from *h*

all that I crave of the for all my service
is to congratulat my gentle spouse
& thou Alcestes sonne Hypodeles
kinge of the wynds pen Close thy rough facte storms
wthin theyr craygy Cavarnes, that our passage
may as our mynds are gently Calme remayne
till we arive one brittish shore againe
Enter Ang:
Ang deare knight make hast the night wth sable winge
whirles forward & I feare me swifter day
will stop our iourney $\overset{r}{p}$thee hast away
are not yo^{rs} followers yet returnde
Red: not yet
Oh I dare pawne my life Anglitora
the slougard Rusticanoes still asleep
Ile call him, Rusticano, ho Rusticano
he speaks wthin
Ru: why doe ye call me at this time of night, what avengeans ayle [Fol. 38a]
yo^{v} trowe⟨:⟩ I know my vather will not goe to plow these
two howrs yet, pray let me alone
Ang: He thinks he is at home wth his father
Red: I soe a does, peace alitle, rise sluggard, rise for
shame away to ship
Rus: will yo^{w} nere ha done wth a murren to ye, I say yt
is not tyme to goe to field with the sheep these iije howres
yet
Red: What a grooms this sirrha rise wth speed, or weel
leave thee still in this lande
Ru: yfayth if I were neare y$\overset{v}{o}$ Ide throw a bedstafe
at yor heade, talke not to me of lande: a man cannot
see to fallow the lande at this time of night
Red: This will not doe Ile trie an other means ho Ru:
the paps hot hears a great messe of milke stayes the eating⟨e⟩
if yo^{u} will not come quickly yor fellow will eat yt from y$\overset{w}{o}$
Ru: O for gods sake looke toot a litle, Ile make me ready. as
soone as eu*er* I can⟨.⟩ I Come, I Come
Red: I marry sir I thought this would get him vp, if any
thinge could, credit me Ang: hees as tall a trencher

2444 *spouse*] *p* ? altered 2445 *Alcestes*] *l* altered *Hypodeles*] ? for *Hypotades* 2447 *craygy*] ^{1}*y* perhaps meant for *g* 2449 *we*] *w* begun as *c* *arive*] *v* altered 2451 *winge*] *e* ends in flourish resembling , 2454 *yet*] *e* altered from first stroke of *t* 2455 *not*] *o* altered or blotted 2459 *he*] *h* altered from long *s* 2460 *doe*] *e* blotted or altered 2470 *still*] *s* ? altered 2476 *yt*] letters amalgamated 2477 *looke*] *l* altered 2478 *can*] *n* has three minims 2480 *credit*] *c* altered from *e* *tall*] *ta* altered from *goo*

man as any in all Europ, peace hear he Comes in hast
now Rusticano
Ru: A poyson take yo^{w} m^{r} are yo^{w} there, are these yor tricks
yo^{w} have more then are good I see:
Red, Come sirrha leave these triflings hence away
are all our Company at hande
Om: we are Enter Company
Red Come sweet Ang: like fortunes share
Ang: wth all my heart sweet rose, great land adewe
I feare me my dep*ar*ture thow wilt rue
parents forgiue me, parents fare ye well
love p*ro*ves to some a heaven to some hell (xeunt
Red Come fayrest princesse
Enter Prester Iohn and his queene in theyre night
habiliments
Q: How fares my lord, what maks yo^{w} thus to rise [Fol. 38b]
before the Chearfull larke, what are yo^{w} well
are yo^{w} in health my liege, I pray yo^{v} tell
I ran to follow yo^{w}, somethings amisse
hath ought disturbde yor rest, doth ought p*er*plex ye
P yt doth sweet ((Bellamy) introth yt doth
I dreamde the fearfullst & heart masinge dreme
as that the thought oft was so hidious
yt did awake my senses, since wich tnye
by noe means Could I entertayne this slumber
such terrour did yt strike vnto my sowle
the very thought oft doth still amaze me
me thought I stood vpon a Craggy rocke
invironde wth the oceans raginge waves
from whence I did behold a g⟨o⟩odly ship
gallauntly rigd & mande, & as I gazde
vpon that obiecte, who there should I see
vpon the hatches but Anglittora
in folded in the armes of Arthures knight
when callinge to her straight me thoughts she smylde
& bid me neu*er* more expect my Chylde
addinge more ou*er* that the Redrose knight

2482 *Rusticano*] *R* altered from *r* 2485 *sirrha*] *i* unformed, though dot is present *hence*] *c* altered from *e* 2489 *rose,*] *e* added above , *land*] *l* altered, ? from *c* 2492 *(xeunt*] (, ? *C* 2493 *fayrest*] *y* altered from *r* 2496 *my*] *m* ? blotted or altered 2500 *doth*] *h* altered or added 2501 ^{1}*yt*] altered from *He* ^{2}*yt*] altered from *he* 2502 *dreme*] first element of *m* resembles *a* 2504 *did*] ^{1}*d* begun as ? *w* *tnye*] dot over *y* suggests *time* was intended 2505 *by*] altered 2506 *did*] altered *sowle*] *w* started as ? *l* 2507 *very*] *v* altered from *f* 2510 *ship*] *i* has initial ascending loop 2512 *obiecte*] *i* blotted or altered 2513 *vpon*] *v* altered, ? from *C* 2516 *expect*] ^{1}*e* altered, ? from *w*

& she, were copte in Hymeneall league
wich when I sawe, (o lord) such pangs such griefe, [to]
together mixt wth rage did wound my soule
as that (stroak dead wth anguish) thence I fell
into the sea rough boreas maks to swell
and strouglinge there some litle space at laste
death wonne the victory, lifes strength was past
Q: heavens p*ro*tecte yor sacred mats
from such blacke fatall Infortunity
P did yov not heare me sheuer nor start, nor shrinke
Q most fearfully my lord, o'
P: Oh Bellamy
the gods defend vs from such mysery
weele looke more Carefull to or daughters steps
“ yovths soone will tread awry vnless there stande
“ discretions proppe to guide it by the hand [FOL. 39a]
but yet my soule can neuer entertaine
an Ethiops scandall or base thought of him
that tare the dragon peecemeale limme from limme Enter a lo:
Lo: My liedge
P: Speake why dost weepe why doth thine eies
pruent thy tongue, what infelicities
haue now betide vs?
Lo: Oh my lord yor daughter
P: why what of her speake briefely
Lo: Oh shees gone
gone wth the Red Rose Knight some 3 houres since
shipt hence away and now th'aue cut the seas
past past'recalling
prest: Oh ingratefull Child
Runne, fly pursue and follow them returne not
till they returne raise all the coast and countrey
seeke euery monarches court to find them out
o thankles child, o ingratefull brittaine
did I for this bestow such fauors on thee
did I for this giue thee such entertaine
did I for this honor the britaines soe

2519 *wich*] *i* formed as *c* but dotted 2520 *wound*] *d* altered 2521 *stroak*] *r* formed as *e* 2524 *lifes*] *s* added
2525 *yor*] *r* altered from *w* 2527 *yov*] extra loop above *y*, *v* imperfectly formed *sheuer*] [1]*e* added *shrinke*] *i* added
2531 *daughters*] *d* altered from *b*; *te* amalgamated
2533–2605 Hand D 2534 *can*] *a* resembles *u* 2538 *weepe*] *w* altered, ? from long *s* 2539 *infelicities*] [1]*e* blotted
2546 *past'recalling*] *p* formed as abbreviation for *pro* 2548 *pursue*] *p* formed as abbreviation for *pro*

to robbe, depriue mee of my life, my ioy
degenerate brittaines brutish now indeed
wherein had I deserued this at yor hands
or how had p: I: proued soe ingrate
that you should plague him thus o gentle girle
I trust thou tenderst more thy parents age
I know thou hast more pittie in thy brest
then to foresake vs craz'd and worne wth [age] yeares
sweete wench retourne see how thy mother mournes
at thy disloyall flight, let teares constraine
thine adamantine heart to some remorse
if not our time-spent yeares o thinke what pangs
and carefull throwes thy mother bare for thee
then leaue her not in such vile miserie
Q: Mild Neptune force her hither backe againe
Th⟨ou⟩ so⟨nn⟩e of Cælum wafte her backe againe
Trump-sounding Triton bring her backe againe [Fol. 39b]
yee Dryades conduct her backe[⟨.⟩] againe
Sterne Æolus o whirle her backe againe
Earth, water, ayre, fire, all yee all
bring, send, wafte and compell her to returne
for whom in passion thus wee sighe and mourne Enter Lo:
Lo: wee cannot heare of them the siluer streames
runne smooth and glasse-like and the dolphins play
on the seas billowes:
p: Oh blacke dismall day
And can Anglitora proue so vngrate
vnto her carefull parents loue farewell
hate thee Ile entertaine yee gods geeue eare
Deformed mishapen vgly sterne abortiue
let their ingratefull issue dastard, brat
if euer they haue any proue most hideous
affright the mother at his luckeles birth
and let him liue to proue vnto her soule
as kind as euer shee hath beene to mee
nay let him liue to bee her vtter ruine
heauen I pray yo^{u} heare a little more
let that disloyall knight y^{t} rap't her hence
dye by the hands of his now loued trull
then shall our torments bee reuenged at full

2567 *throwes*] *t* ? added 2568 *miserie*] ^{2}*e* has final flourish

2 Lo: Oh cease thes direfull execra$\overline{cons}$ lord
yor spirits swaied by rage mad phrenzyes child
p: No, could I but inuent more horrid curses
could I but belch out direr impreca$\overline{cons}$
Ide vp wth all.
1 Lo: my liedge twere very well
to rid your stomacke of them they resemble
" and likest are vnto an orbicke ball
" wch first [thr]strikes him that [that] threw it against the wall.
p: No more I chardge yo^{u} come (sweet Bellamy)
accurse thy daughters blacke impiety/

Q: looke ye doe ye see this one my princes word it is as good to bring vppe a calfe [FOL. 40a] as a daughter, that will neu*er* for sake the dame, this doth a daughter, why all ye world can witnes how dearelie I tender'd her, how care full I was of her I would no^{t} soe much as suff⟨er⟩ the wind to blowe on her, yet doth shee most vnnaturally, leaue her ever care full mother, what an vnkind woman am I to accuse my pretty girle thus, noe twas that purblind boy that [top o]hop on my thumbe, Cupid I meane, twas he that stole away my Childs heart & when that was onc^{e} gone shee must needs followe, ho la, looke, heers Hecate heeres proserpine, ye false hearte⟨.⟩ trull, could yo^{u} bee soe obdurate, soe unpassionate, to bereaue me of my gentle daughter, it ioyes me it that I haue met wth yo^{u}, Ile tugge, Ile dragge, Ile grapple wth yo^{u} for all yor magicke spells and blacke incantations, wast yo^{u} m^{rs} Cinthia, wch made my daughter run [o]away wth a base Brittaine fugitiue, noe forged excuse shall saue yo^{u} from my fury: thus thus Ile auenge my self. { shee drawes one of the ladyes by the haire of the head along the stag^{e}/

p: Sweet Q: why are thy thoughts distemperd thus
that pleasing voice was wont to yeeld more comfort

Q: A cole blacke crowe this morne peep'd in my face. & an hideous runey crosst the way before me, the derne skritchowll beate at my casem^{t} windowe, wth such horrid amazem^{t}, & amazing terror, as all the world may knowe they bore me some ominous will, & see like to so⟨m⟩e skilfull prognosticatrs they foretold these maleuolent aspects. & ill pertending prodigyes, they haue more wit then all yo^{u} haue, [here] haue, after yo^{u} most leardied astrologers haue after yo^{u}. Exit./

2601 *your*] *y* added
2606–2704 Hand C 2607 *the*] *th* malformed 2608 *world*] *ld* altered from *d* 2611 *my*] *y* retraced in darker ink ^{2}*that*] *a* altered or retraced 2623 *voice*] *v* and *c* altered *yeeld*] *l* ? altered *more*] ascender before *m* 2625 *runey*] *y* retraced; ? for *cuney* 2629 *maleuolent*] *n* altered 2630 *leardied*] ^{1}*d* added

P: Be gracious to her ye celestiall spirits
Robbe her not of her intellectuall powers
o charme my sencs in a lasting sleepe
let m⟨y⟩ mortality be made imortall
by bearing more then ever mortall did
ding downe my soule lower then hells abysse
Rather then i⟨n⟩e feele those miseryes [FOL. 40b]
I ame decrepit & old crazed & stiff
why put yo^{u} then the hugest massy lode
vpon the most vnable to sustaine it
old age is weakest, if plagues needes must fall
my youth Could best haue borne & suffred all
oh lay a Chaos of confusion on me
ells shall I deeme yor iudgemts most iniust
let dust returne from whenc^{e} [t] it Came to dust——Entr Lo:
Lo: My liege I bring yo^{u} sole sad newes the queene
distract & senceles ran orethwart the meades
decking her head wth cockle, fearne-locke tares
that growe dispersed one the Campion plaine
mixt teares wth smiles shee ecchoes furth this note
as burthen to her swanlike mourne full song
my daughter sweet Ang: is gone
and to a swift-hed torrent comes at last
wherein shee casts her self. oh not her self
her garments bare her one the silu*er* streame
meane while shee senceles of her misery
sate warbling furth the pleasantst notes shee could
ere helpe could succur her shee layed her head
vpon the riu*er*s bosome sanke & dyed
P O let the bases & foundation sinke
of this terrestriall tripartited globe
that everlastinge silenc^{e} may orewhelme
my wofull self in deepest barathrum
why are soe incensd ye sacred powers
to heape yor ponderous iudgem^{ts} on my head
a[h] poore old man ye see vnapt to beare
o strike me wth yor thunder, let not yre
be two secure thus f⟨or⟩cing me to feele
and see such fatall vile disastrous acts

2632 *spirits*] ^{1}*i* formed as *r* but dotted 2633 *intellectuall*] ^{1}*l* altered or retraced 2637 *abysse*] *y* dotted 2638 *i⟨n⟩e*] ? for *ile* 2639 *crazed*] *d* added 2647 *yo^{u}*] *y* altered from long *s* 2651 *teares*] *t* altered from *l* 2660 *dyed*] *y* altered, ? from *e* 2661 *the*] *e* altered from *i* 2665 *are*] ? for *are ye* 2669 *two*] *o* altered or added

will yee not pitty see ile d⟨o⟩e it my self
Behold ye frowning heauens I disdaine [FOL. 41a]
to breath one minute longer in [di]such payne,—— he stabbs himself
Mount, mount, my soule, & meet thy glorious consort then staggers & speaks
hovering in the ayre, & [⟨b⟩]looke the eternall essence
spreads it self to imbrace thee, looke it stayes
fly, fly my spiritt see, see, heere I haue giuen thee
free passage from thy fleshes loathsome [dange⟨r⟩] dungeon
why stayest thou, sword thy manumission's bought
thy freedomes purchast wth my dearest blood
close eyes, stoppe eares, tongue cleaue vnto thy Roofe
cease, cease, you weake supporters: proppe me not
let all the powers of decoying nature
be frozen senceles, stupid stiffe, benumbd
Strong heart resist not powerfull facultyes
giue way to meagre, [grim] leane & grim⟨.⟩-fac'd death
let it of sence, of moc̅o̅n̅ cleane bereaue me
frailty adue, adue, thus, thus I leaue thee.————Moritur./
1 Lo: Great Ioue protect our king o see my lords
his soule hath closed her opticke windowes vppe
and left the bodyes mansion
2 Lo: o ye gods
how are ye angry wth vs, in his fall
this kingdome state is ruind & vs all
1 Lo. Come, come in mournefull sort lets beare him hence
for neu*er* region lost a better prince
2 Lo: Lets goe, lets goe, accursed be the hower
we entertaind the Brittaines fatall power

A dead march: they beare the king over the stage mourning, Enter
2 ladyes of fayeria wth Cælia's child in their armes.

1 lady: I much admire how we can misse her grace
Shee ever makes abode about this place
2 lady Pray heavens that noe harme attend her highnes
or that ⟨ ⟩ doe not in some franticke minde./
Caste her selfe headlonge downe this stony rocke [FOL. 41b]
where shee hath sate for lorne at least i2 moones
j La: shee hath indeed, Oh how are wee accurst
that Can not dare [bu]to come, but once each day

2674 *thy*] *y* altered from *e* 2676 *self*] *l* retraced 2679 *sword*] ? for *soul* 2686 *grim*⟨.⟩-] either *m* has four minims, or *e* deleted by hyphen 2695 *mournefull*] [1]*u* altered from *r* 2696 *region*] otiose dash over *n* 2699 *they*] *y* added
2704 Hiatus caused by tear in leaf: missing word probably *shee*
2705–39 Hand A 2707 *La*] *L* altered, ? from *2* 2708 *come*] *m* blotted or altered

vnto her prsens, oh twould grieve mans sowle
to see a princesse that tofore was wise
soe farre mistake her selfe, her Court to fly
leavinge vs wretched in her misery
And s[h]ee shee Comes, good morrow to yor grace

Enter Cælia
pale & wan

2 Health to yor excellens
i La: ioy vnto yor heart
Cæ: Wee thanke yow lovinge subiects, what our Childe
God blesse my boye Come I must kisse thy lips
Ladies I see yor Care, the Childe fares well
Looks iolly prty knave thy sweet ffac'te sight
brings to my mynde thy dad, (the Redrose knight)
but Ladies nowe Ile tell yow what I sawe
this night that paste, I gazde vpon this rocke
& spide his shippe wavinge his Anchoradge
Top and Top Gallaunt hetherward amayne
the Crosse was fixte vpon the stately banner
wch made mee knowe yt was the redrose knight
the Crosse he bears yow knowe, but see Crosse fortune
she steers his Course wth greatest violence
from hence amayne, then did I shout, & Cry
flamde all the beacons, filde each place wth fire
exclaimde, & prayde, & wisht, & roarde, yet all
Could not, o Could not hither them recall
wich when I sawe lord how I wept & cride
and mournde, & sorrowed to be thus denide
but hence & featch some meat, for nowe I sweare
neu*er*, or eu*er* more will I stay heare
both La: Oh ioy intollerable
1 La: In troth tis time
to see yor pallace for yow looke like slime
the basest of all earth, yor cheekes waxe pale [FOL. 42a]
yor face most leane.
Cæ: then am I bad for sale
i La: yor grace is merry
Cæ: yea and iocund too
Ioyfull, and iouiall, lightsome, void of woe.
hence fetch cates, meane while my boy and I

2709 *grieve*] [1]*e* altered from *v* 2712 *her*] *h* altered by addition of descender 2713 *And*] *A* altered from long *s* 2716 *what*] *w* altered from *o* 2720 *dad*] [2]*d* altered from *e* 2730 *fire*] *i* formed by dotting *r* 2735 *featch*] *t* altered from *c* 2738 *troth*] *r* altered from *h*
2740–2845 Hand D

will sit and laugh vpon the grasse here by
Om: weele goe with ioyfull hearts the gods bee praised
that's sorrowes siedge at length by ioy is raised Ex:La:
Cæ: what are they gone? alas they litle knew
how my lords absence still this heart doth rue
and euer shall, since that hee came soe neare
and would not [loue] see his Cælia loues him deare
full deare indeed, and that the end shall proue
how deare I was endear'd vnto his loue
here see here, this lr̄e haue I writte
vnto my lord; my self will carry it shee pulles a lr̄e
for clos'd wthin a seare cloth: and kept sure out of her bosome
from tincture of the water: 'bout this necke
fast will I tye it, this done will I throw
my self into the Ocean: twas my vowe
& Ile obserue it, softe Ile read it o're
(least I should out) this one tyme more she reads the [lre]letter
" vnto the mirrour of all courtesy
" the Red Rose knight bright starre of chivalry
" poore Cælia wishes all the loue shee can
" vnto thee constant, faithfull, loyall man.
" since yor departure hence: I looked still
" yor [m](once made promise) when you would fulfill
" for as yo^{u} know once did you promise mee
" backe to returne in hast right speedily
" these limbes ne're touch't bed since hence you went
" but day and night yea all in greefe I spent
" in cold, in heate, vpon a Rocke I sate:
" expecting thee: that dost poore Cælia hate
" from yesterday, thy happie ship past by.
" wch I then ey'd then did I showte, call, crie, [Fol. 42b]
" implore and threaten, yea great fires light
" could not invite thee hither (noble knight)
" wch seeing, then thy wretched Cælia knew
" thou wast (I dare not say false or vntrue)
" yet most ingratefull: and this caused mee write
" this instant to thee who wa'st my delight
" I am the bearer o let Neptune guide
" this mournefull body to thy princely side

2753 *see*] interlined above deletion with caret 2763 *she*] very cramped, as if *he* added 2776 *from*] ? for *for*
2777 *call*] large flourish above ^{2}l

“ dead or aliue I pray, o mayst thou bee
“ as blest as I am full of misery
“ if either yet infortunate thine owne
“ poore Cælia fayrie Queene and thine alone
“ Soe tis as I would haue it, hearke yee gods
since tis yor will thus to afflict a Queene
that might haue beene more happie had you pleas'd
o heare my latest praier protect my lord
from all ensuing p*er*ills, let his dayes
be lengthned to his comfort, and yor praise
And let this wretched trunke (o all I craue)
rest in his bosome ere it lies in graue.
if hee but shed a teare or two or'e mee
thats all I beg for all my misery
and let his offspring here whome I co̅mend
into yor hands (poore orphants onely freind/
let him I say as magnanimious proue
as euer was his father whome I loue
Adieu sweete boy this is the latest kisse
thy mother e're shall giue thee, troth hee weepes
Alas (poore soule) I will not leaue thee soe
hard hearted Cælia o recall thy vow
see how thy babe intreats thee wth his teares
(tis all the language that an [h] infant hath
whereby hee tells his mother of his wrongs)
o weepe not soe sweete babe mine armes shall lull [Fol. 43a]
thy tender body till thou art asleepe
let mee go looke thy dad, hee weepeth still
“ in slaying of my selfe my babe I kill
but see I trifle, come one kisse and p*ar*te
alas his teares doe strike me to the heart
but I must hast, lye there my pretty boy
my ladies as I trust will nurse my ioy.
Adieu vaine worldly pompe ladies farewell
Adieu bright-shining towres the worldlings ioy
Adieu yee goodly pallaces my boy
thy mother takes her last adieu of thee
o may'st thou proue more happy farre then mee
And last to thee great Brittaines greatest praise
thy freind doth wish eternity of dayes
Life I despise thee welcome long-wisht death

2808 *thee*] 1*e* altered from *y*

thou art my comfort, farewell soone-lost breath
gods take my spirit Neptune on thy brest
safely conduct mee to him I loue best. { shee casts her selfe from the rocke.
Enter 2 ladies wth vittailes running.
1 La: O s[h]ee shee threw her self hence from the rocke
into the bosome of oceanus: [acc⟨ur⟩sed]
Accursed as wee are wee all must hence
giuing her scope vnto this blacke offence
2 La: had wee obserued her words wee might foresee
this fatall acte, and wofull misery.
shee did not say to court shee would returne
but that shee would not any longer mourne
i La: Heauens receaue her teares cannot recall her
wherefore let's cease to weepe, the child Ile take
and in great care instruct it for her sake
2 La: The grauest matrons shall lament her fall
in sable weedes at her blacke funerall
wch weele now solemnise, I lets goe
Eternall woe to them that caused this woe. Ex: Ladies.
Enter tyme [Fol. 43b]
Time heere might end a truelie tragigke play
but that the RedRose knight calls tyme away
sowre mixt wth sweet is good. but onlie sweet
will sooner cly then when they both doe meet
heere for to leaue you were to dip our pen
more deepe in wormewood then in mel, & then
tyme might displease, wch rather then heele doe
our subiect now shall runne noe more of woe
onlie Ile shewe you how faire Cælia came
vnto our English champion valours fame
yor thoughts must once more helpe vs thinke you see
the Redrose knight wthin his ship at sea
where one the lofty hatches he espyes
faire Cælia, see't presented to yor eyes (A dumbe shew
Enter the Red Rose knight & his followers: Ang: to them a marin*er* bearing in a dead body: the Red Rose knight vieweth her seriously: knowes her for Cæ: he makes great tokens of sorrowe, & all weepe, sr Gallowyne espyes a string about her necke, when pulling it out, the Red: reedes it & maks great lamentation: they beare out the body & Exeunt./

2846–2906 Hand C 2847 *truelie*] *r* altered from *o* 2850 *cly*] ? for *cloy* 2856 *vnto*] *v* altered from *o* *our*] *o* altered from *v* 2858 *sea*] *a* altered from *e* 2860 *eyes*] [1]*e* smudged 2864 *necke*] *k* altered or retraced

Thus sayling one the sea the Red Rose knight
sees a dead [knight] truncke, tosst by the ocean waues
Richly attyred and the mr calls
to hale it vppe wch as soone effected
as [s]hee requir'd it when wth serious eye
he quickly calls to mind faire Cælia
& knew her liuelie phisiognomy
her comely lineaments & then his heart
proued him as guilty of her present death
thus grieuing good sr Gallowyne espyes
the string to wch the l̅r̅e̅ fast was tyed
pulling it furth the Red Rose knight doeth see
contained therein her loyall constancy
wch greatly did assault he manlike breast
& made it stoope to passion voyed of Rest
Time now must turne his scene to [Englands] Brittaines bownds
whether full shortlie shall our knights arriue [FOL. 44a]
now passeth he the Cost of much fame'd france
but leauing him; to Arthur weele returne
whoe in his absence many famous acts
& dreadfull warrs against the Saxons waged
& hee theire ragefull fury much asswaged
yet never, quite extinguishd what befell
by yor attentiue silence he shall tell Ex:———

Sownd: Enter k: Arthur, Q: Gwiniver, Androgeo: sr lamorake, sr palamed⟨e⟩

k: Arth: welcome braue knights at yor appointed time &c⟨.⟩
to repossesse yor seats of Pentecost
wch is the tyme all knights that doe belong⟨:⟩
vnto our table[⟨s⟩] ought to hast wth speed
weele feast, most Royally for this we knowe
The world shall never such a table showe

Q: – my L: yor maiesty are[⟨.⟩] welcome home
vnto yor loving Gwiniver, yor warres
& well fought battailes, wch yor grace hath wag'd
not only gainst the Saxons & the french
but wth the lofty Romanes whoe excell
in feats of armes as historyes can tell
yor victoryes I say against them all

2869 *vppe*] *v* altered from *p* *as*] ? for *was as* 2874 *death*] *e* formed from deleted letter, ? *o* 2879 *he*] ? for *his* 2880 *passion*] final flourish of *n* suggests , 2881 *Brittaines*] interlined above deletion 2884 *Arthur*] *u* lacks minim 2888 *never*] *v* altered, ? from *d*

hath beene the cause we never could enioye
twin'd in those ar⟨m⟩es nor for a twelue moneth space
in modest sort each other loues embrace.
K: Ar: The end shall pay for all (sweete Gwiniuer)
yet trust mee lords, it glads yor sou*er*aignes soule
to thinke wth what vnequall hardiment
wee put to flight the Romane generall
thou Lamoracke didst coope the Romane leader
three times together: nor could hee wthstand
the euerponderous blowes of that high-hand
his nephew pallomede thrice ouerthrew
all fought right gallant weele giue each his due.
Lam: yor highnes pleaseth for to speake our praise
yet are wee most vnworthy of such fame. It is yor honor merits valours name
k: noe more of that. Androgeo honour'd earle [FOL. 44b]
how welcome art thou to thy sou*er*aign's cort
to Camelot thrice welcome hast thou viewed
as tis thine vse the seats of all our knights
And: I haue ant please yor highnes excellence
k: how many seats of fifty are there voyed
And: But foure of them renowned liege
k: wch are they
And: sr Trist: Lance. & sr Gall:
and he thats farre degreed aboue them all
the Red Rose knight o should he chaunce to fall
by some malevolent planet in his trauell
the forme would totter wch is now infract
the french rebell by other nations back'd
k: O now thou rubst a long since grieuous skarre
and being chaf't you make it vexe the more
the Redrose knight? forgieve me memory
hence dull oblivion of his Chivalry
didst neu*er* heare or any of yow all
what Countreys he hath Coasted
Pall: yes great lord
Pallomides hath heard in fraunce & Spayne

2905 *ar⟨m⟩es*] *m* blotted or altered
2907–17 Hand D 2914 *his*] *i* ? added
2918–33 Hand C 2918 *Androgeo*] *g* altered or retraced 2919 *how*] *w* altered, ? from *n* *welcome*] *l* altered from *c* 2920 *viewed*] *v* altered or retraced 2922 *ant*] *t* altered from *c* 2927 *farre*] ²*r* altered from *d* 2930 *would*] *l* altered from *d* *infract*] *c* altered from *k* 2932 *skarre*] ²*r* altered from *e* 2933 *you*] *y* altered from *t*
2934–3095 Hand A 2935 *Chivalry*] *r* altered from *y* 2939 *heard*] *r* interlined

how he yor spotles honour did mayntaine
nay in yor name vnhoarst all durst wthstand
yor name or fame wthin the Sophies land
of Royall Persia

K Ar: O lords twas a knight
blest in successe, succesfull, in attempts
attemptinge nothinge but he did acheeve
atchievinge nothinge but wth blazde renowne
renowninge honour, honouringe his name
nam'd neu*er* but with prayes & endless fame
his acts are such a Chaos that I wante
Some smoothd tonge Cicero wch might Compose
& frame them wth some methodizinge stile [FOL. 45a]
for loe I ende begininge all this while

Enter Poast

Po: my liege

K Some news of him most gratious heavens

Po: The redrose knight with gallant pomps at hande
wth all his troupe returnde, not one man lost
though often as I know he hath bene Crost
He came disguised wth his Company
Cause non showld certify yor maiesty
onely remaynes in Cort me sends before
to see yf yowle admitte them

K Oh ye gods are yo^{w} soe happyly p*ro*pitious
to least deservinge Arthure: welcome him?
yes if our Court kept here at winchester
Can gieve them entertayne: admitte them lords,

Enter Rus: disguised like the Red: Ang: Gall, L: Tr: following him the kinge runs & embraceth him

K O blessed hower, O thrise happy time
Brave Tom A Lincolne, welcome to our Clime

Rus: I am as glad to see yor worships grace
as for to see a Cup of ale before my face

Q: thus doth the queene: although my lords in viwe
not hand but mouth affoord

Rus: Ile take yt of yo^{w}
& for the same, I tell yo^{w} queene againe
I kist yo^{w} once before this nowe maks twayne

Good lord doe not yo^{w} knowe me: why twas I gave yo^{w} the smacke ore the lips a great while agoe, lord how forgetfull yo^{w} are? my names

2942 *yor*] *y* altered, ? from *n* 2945 *blest*] *l* ? added 2949 *prayes*] *e*, ? *r* 2952 *frame*] *r* altered from *a* 2959 *He*] *H* altered from *L* 2967 *Ang:*] *g* retraced or altered 2975 *Ile*] *l* altered, ? from *e* 2977 *once*] *c* altered from *e*

Rus: the travelour: & how doe yo^{w} m^{r} kinge karter, & m^{rs} queene Miniver
K how darst delude vs thus: whers thy m^{r} speake
Ru: O lord sir: straunge fortune hath befalne him in his adventurs: he is metamorphosed into a poast: & yet Ile tell yo^{w} stranger newes then y⟨t⟩ this poast quatenus poast, did yo^{w} heare speake fore any of vs knigh⟨t.⟩ of the rownd table, that yo^{w} are newly returned into England,
Nay? wich is a marvayle of all Mervayles: this poast hath maried [Fol. 45b]
one of the p^{r}tiest lasses in the world: & yo^{w} know tis a simple
wench will lie wth a poast
Kinge: Either thow speakst Ænigmaes or delirem^{ts}, Come p^{r}thee
resolve vs be our Œdipus
Ru: I know not what yor Edib*us* is, but whereas I sayde o^{r} m^{r} was
turned into a poast, tis trewe & this poaste y^{t} brought yo^{w} news
of o^{r} returne is he: I pray yo^{w} did not he speake to yo^{w}, before
we sawe yo^{w}: I sayde moreou*er* that this poast had maried one of the
p^{r}tiest lasses in the versall worlde: how say yo^{w} by this lady
is it not a p^{r}tty peece of flesh? have I satisfied yo^{w} now trowe?
K. Is this our royall knight? He descou*er*s him selfe
Red Great lord I am,
And cravinge p*ar*done of yor maiesty, (they kneele)
for this our Com̄ick iest: on bended knee
wee humble thus our selves: in all o^{r}. search
I Could not fynde a father, onely see
my seconde selfe, Ioynde nearest vnto mee
if all my weake deserts, doe m*er*it grace
graunte me one small request
K: yes werte to place
in state, & rayse thee to our regall [s⟨ta⟩] throne
what ere thow dost demaunde yt is thine owne
Red the like I beg of yo^{w} great sou*er*aignesse
Q Our ears are open to what ere yt be
& will accept yt
Red: O felicity
how highly hast thow raysde me? first I Crave
I this great princesse to my wiefe may have
next that yor highnes wth yor noble queene
will entertayne her as yt best[st] beseeme
the sole inheretrix of that great lande
wich Prester Iohn now rules & that yor hand

2982 *adventurs*] *v* altered 2989 *or*] *r* altered, ? from *n* 2990 *Œdipus*] *Œ* written over start for *Æ* 2992 *trewe*] ^{1}e altered from *i* 2994 *the*] *t* altered from *c* 2997 *He*] *H* altered from *h* 3007 *regall*] *e* altered from *o* 3016 *best[st]*] ^{1}t altered 3018 *yor*] blot or deletion above *y*

will royally Combine our soles in one
makinge of two a p*er*fect vnion

K Q — what are yo^{w} pleasde [high] great Princesse

Ang: — were I not
yo^{w} neu*er* showld have tyde this Gordian knott

K: — knights yo^{w} are welcome all, our Court shall shew [FOL. 46a]
Kinge Arthures bownty neu*er* flowde till nowe
wele first $\overset{r}{p}$pare for Nuptialls then for sports
next shall yo^{w} tell what hapte y$\overset{w}{o}$ in kings Courts

Red — Nowe let vs see how yo^{w} kinde Countreymen
Congratulate our salph returne againe
if yo^{w} speake welcome, seal yt wth the cryes
if yor aplauses & shrill plaudities [Exeunt om:

Enter Kinge and Andr: leadinge Ang: then enter queen and a lady ledinge Red: knights of the rownde table and other followinge

A songe: [y] ye sacred powers wch rule the skies
Cast downe, cast downe y$\overset{r}{o}$ gratious eyes
vpon this sweet vnited payre
Give both all blisse, give both an heyre
give both &c
an heyre of his fathers mighte
an heyre of his mothers forme
a brave Couragious valiant knight
let vertues selfe this babe adorne
Let vertues &c
And thow great Hymens nuptiall springe
o blesse this happy vnion heere
soe prayrs & himmes we will all singe
vnto thy deyty most deare
vnto thy deyty &c
braue Red rose knight, embrace thy love
fayre princesse love thy princely lorde
as faythfull as the turtle dove
by day by night at bed at boord
by day &c
Braue Arthur thow dost know thy sonne
wich ioyes thee much though thow Conceale yt
but yet before thy glasses runne
to his great griefe thou wilt reveale yt

3029 *salph*] *p* altered from *h* 3030 *the*] *h* altered 3032 *Andr*] *r* altered, ? from *:* 3039 *mighte*] *e* altered from *s* 3044 *springe*] *e* altered from *s* 3045 *heere*] ²*e* altered, ? from *a* 3053 *day*] *a* altered

but peace vayne tongue that bablst soe
yt nought befitts this sacred mirth
goe one, goe one, & as they goe
be ioyfull heaven be frolicke earth
The Epilogue [Fol. 46b]

Thus is the mariage finisht & our play
but whether well or ill wee dare not say
selfe Cusinge Consciens, soone would guilty Cry
but thats againste selfe-lovinge pollicy
first we must be convicted, then Confesse
our skilles arte, our artles guiltines.
the barres the stage, the men arraigned wee
yor Censures are our iudges, oh let them bee
milde, gentle, gracious, not to stricte, to sower
to full of p*er*cinge gall, oh doe not lower
at these our weake indevors: but let love
goe hande in hand wth iudgem^{t}: yea reprove
whats done amisse but yet in such a strayne
as that wee may be sure yor loves remayne
as Constant as before: Our harmelesse sport
our Commicke mirth wee knowe Comes farre to short
& fitts not yor attention: yet the mynde
of eu*ery* actor came noe iott behinde
nor was defective, wherefore (Courteous hearers
Our Author and the Actors here have sent me
to knowe what yo^{w} determine, yea thy sweare
poore Rusticano all the blame shall beare
because he was soe foolish at the vpshotte
to, weare his m^{r}s habit, & to come
soe vnexpected in his leaders roome
(wich as they think is most distastfull to yo^{w}
Wherfore amazde poore Rusticano stands
hopinge yo^{w} will revive him with yor hands
Exit

finis Deo soli gloria
Quam p*er*fecta manent, strenuo p*er*fecta labore
Metra quid exornat? lima, litura, labor
Morganus: Evans:

3059 Mark in right margin 3065 *Consciens*] *c* altered or blotted 3067 *first*] *i* formed as *r* with dot 3080 *came*] *c* altered, ? from *a* 3083 *thy*] ? for *they*

OTHER ITEMS IN THE MANUSCRIPT

[Blank] [Fol. 47a]

[Blank] [Fol. 47b]

Poynts to be observed by my fathers directions [Fol. 48a]

1 Inprimis where Moris Iones hath not Atturned . . tenaunt vnto my father for can dw poub where xijd rent is reserved: vpon Moris lease & he to pay the Chiefe rent of that ground dur-ing the lease I must enquier of Councel learned whether I shall lose but the xijd rent & what will become of the inheritans, quere de hoc theres a fine levied of the lands by Richard Ednevet & his wief vnto me wch they would Crosse if they Cowld/

2 If Richard Ednevet will take x^{ls} & abatem^{t} of all reckonings due vnto me & make a gen*er*all release or acquittance wth word to release errours in all fines by him & his wief acknowledged then pay him the xls & looke for the ould writings of Cwmgwernog they are at pawne at Lewis ap Owens howse of bushop Castle

3 Theyre be three exemplifications of [a]3 fines betweene Richard Ednevet & my father to be sued foorth in Convenient tyme from the pr⟨.⟩mi⟨.⟩tory be acknowledged wthin this [1]2 or 3 years the eldest they will Cost mls apeece at the least & they must be spoken for a sessions before hand to be made ready by the clearke at once enquire whether there be a barre in the last fine, & the nature of a bare & how to avoy⟨d⟩

1 *Poynts*] scribbled *I* above and before *P* 3 *tenaunt*] *un* has three minims 7 *xijd*] interlined 12 *If*] *I* altered, ? from *f* 15 *in all fines*] interlined with caret 21 *exemplifications*] *f* altered from *c* 27 *spoken*] *en* added in paler ink

[Fol. 48b]

Catherin lloyd & her daughter doe bragge that they will have the lan̄ds to wynifreed: her clayme is nothing worth: for after her mother Lucy [I] elopped from her howsband Richard Ednevett she lived in adultery for a long tyme wth Rich: Price who begate winifreed vpon the body of lucy; After wards Richard Ednevett & lucy were reconciled and Content to live as man & wief: then Dauid Thomas Ien: lucy herefather for the setling of his inheritance in lucy & Rich: Edne; & to barre winifreed made a feofm^{t} by the advise of m^{r} Edward Morgan wch is in keepinge wth Edward lloyd whereby the lands are conveyd to lucy & Rich: Ednevot and her heyres begotte from thenceforth by Rich: Ednevett (vz) to the first sonne & the heyres of his body & soe to a number of sonnes, & in default of sonnes to daughters thencforth to be begotten [t]here is neyther sonne nor daughter borne since & my assurancs are made by the advise of m^{r} Iohn lloyd of Ryswyn if wynifreed stirre or before you may have Comission from the hy Cort of Chauncery to call her in to examen witnes, in p*er*petuam reimemoriam & soe p*ro*ve that she was borne in adultery before the feofm^{t} [Fol. 49a] & there fore can have nothinge by the feofm^{t} although the lawe would allow her to be the daughter of Richard Ednevet./ I take yt that Kathern lloyd is payd all her dower for the Ty tan y lan, enquire whe ther ⟨tha⟩t be true or whether she doth clay⟨m⟩ v^{e} ⟨gr⟩oats I must agre wth her for her dower in that ground before the lease be

34 *Lucy*] *y* altered or retraced 40 *live*] *e* formed as *t* 41 *wief* :] : has three dots *then*] *t* retraced 42 *lucy*] followed by vertical stroke *of*] added in paler ink 46 *keepinge*] ^{3}*e* added 48 *Ednevot*] *o* (?*e*) added 50 ^{2}*the*] interlined 60 *in*] four minims *reimemoriam*] ^{1}*i* added *&*] written over false start 66 *tan*] *t* altered, ? from *c* 67–8 ⟨*tha*⟩ . . ⟨*gr*⟩*oats*] *tha* and *gr* defaced by blot

expired wch endureth but 2 crops at[h] the most. | & soe bwy out her dower & doe not rent that grownde to the widow Harbert for she will spoyle all. but gett her barde from sellinge of ale wch is soone donne & threatninge to complayne vpon the iustices of peace for sufferinge her to sell ale in an vnfitt place neare the mountayne side: two miles & more from church where she keeps bad rule & stays many of the mountayne men from coming to church vpon sundayes and hollydays William Barker is to continue in his living vntill o^{r} Lady day & hath payde his rent due at Michaelmas saving tenne groats. and he sayeth he must goe out free at o^{r} Lady day if he hath payd at the entrance or he must:

[Fol. 49b]

Evan ap Lewis and Griffith dauid Bowen are to be dea^{l}t wth all accordinge to theyre leases./ yet they will bestow a Cow or heyfer apeece vpon me to acknowle dge me to be theyre Landlord./

ffor the meadowe bought of Dauid Ienkin [called] [Tir] neer Calbioch Dauid is bownd to acknowledg a fyne wch I thought would have served my turne but now he sayth that his f [wief] fine & his wieves are nothinge worth & if there weare a feofm^{t} made to Edward Dauid Ienkin his mother being the first wief of Dauid. then a release from Edw: must be had of all his title & claym wch may be optained for a litle or nothing specially if I deale wth my vncle Ienkin lloyd: my father lent Edw: v^{s} Coming from londaine & stayd for payn^{t} a good while and

72 *grownde*] *w* altered from *m* 76 *of*] preceded by false start, ? long *s* 81 *sundayes*] *n* altered from *d* 85 *and*] *a* altered from false start 90 *they*] *ey* altered from *l* 91 *acknowle*] *k* altered from *c* 94 *neer*] interlined above deletion 97 *f*] interlined above deletion *wieves*] *v* altered from *f* 103 *for*] *f* altered from *o* 107 *and*] altered

Dauid Ienkin was Contented to
stop that & gieve him a litle more
& he would seal a release./ theres
all the Challenge and incombrance
that I knowe vpon my lands

i6i6 [FOL. 50a]

Merthines Prophysyes translated:
Of the twelve moneths, of the plannets-
that raygne in eu*er*y moneth, the nature
and fortunes of them that are borne in
them And

[FOL. 50b]

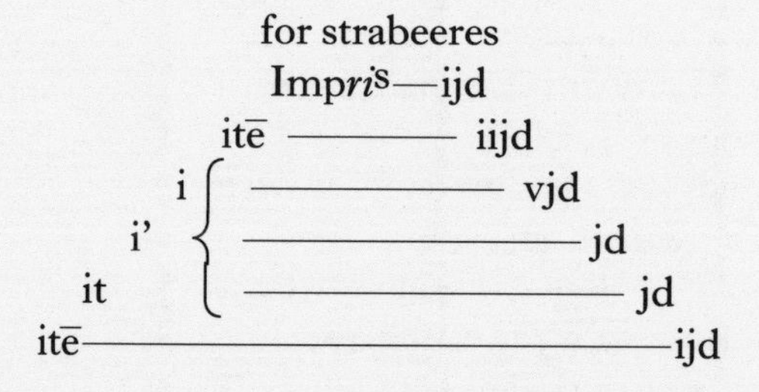

i6i9 [FOL. 51a]

Merthines destinies translated

from mid Ianuary to mid ffrebruary

[FOL. 51b]

such is the force of Beuty ioynde with worth
that from all subiects yt can thus bringe foorth
effects of wonder: I that did nere knowe
a lovinge passion, onely what I owe
to parents, and [the like] my friends, nor, eu*er* thought
a constant harte shoulde be by passion wrought
soe soone to change, [I thes] that nowe alas I p*ro*ve

FOL. 50b 5–7 First word heavily blotted and unclear: blots also visible on fol. 51a.
FOL. 51a Pen tests below text
FOL. 51b Hand appears not to be A 2 *thus*] *th* heavily blotted 3 *nere*] *re* altered from *u'* 5 *my friends*] interlined above deletion 7 *that* and *alas*] both interlined

____

the sacred power of bewty begetts love
and [fownded] wear⟨e⟩d on that rocke yt doth aspire
as high as is the element of fire
without all other growndworke, [nor yst the frown] soe [and] I fynde
[of winde ore thunder that can blowe yt downe]
that [bewty] passion beyand nature turnes the mynde
[⟨on⟩] wheeles of change, [whence I see] wich cherisht in the thought
[yt is a substance of æternity]
______________________________ I that thought not at all
on anay love but what was naturall
and brought vp with me,
but like the flame of a well [like] builded fire
[made of cælestiall matter, since w]
being by woode suprest doth mount the higher

[Missing] [Fols. 52–56]

[Blank] [Fols. 57a–58a]

when she is angry with some whore then p*ro*ve her [Fol. 58b]
and tell her thoult revenge that soe dost love her
the Chambermayde a mornings will not fayle
to put the rowers helpe vnto the sayle
and muttringly sheel say, mistres yow can
neu*er* I thinke enough requite that man
then she will prayse p*er*swade intreat to save
ells that her love will bringe thee to thy grave

[Missing] [Fol. 59]

Fayere yonge man be content, [Fol. 60a]
A waye with sighes and wepings,
Doe not your selves torment,
In cares and sorrowes keepinge,
For it was neuer seene soe faiere a spoken yonge man,,

9 *wear⟨e⟩d*] interlined above deletion 9–10 marked for deletion by two pairs of vertical strokes 11–12 marked for deletion by one pair of vertical strokes 11 *soe . . . fynde*] interlined above with caret 13 *that*] *at*, ? *us* *passion*] interlined above deletion 14 *see*] ^{1}*e* altered from *h* *wich . . . thought*] interlined above with caret 19 *well*] altered from . *hot* *builded*] interlined above deletion 21 *woode*] ^{2}*o* altered from *d*

Fol. 58b Hand A? 2 *revenge*] *v* altered, ? from *e* 3 *not*] *no* altered from *w* 4 *put*] *p* altered from *t* *rowers*] *e* altered from *r*

Fols. 60a–61a Hand not found elsewhere in manuscript 5 *yonge man,*] interlined above, with caret beneath *o* in *spoken*

But euer hath there bine more false desemling
woman

The voues which shee protested,
To loue [thee] mee aboue [m]any,
Nou doe I finde shee Iested,
For shee loues to to many.
Shee prayeth when shee left mee,
Shee neuer might come amonge men,
O that shuch flatring hartes should be,
Amonge shuch proper women,

Her outward forme and shape,
By natur was well framed,
But her desemling harte,
Her comely makeing shamed,
But o that false delight,
Soe much should euer wronge men,
As her false hart hath done to mee,
Beinge wronged by a woman

O that shuch shugred wordes, [Fol. 60b]
Should foulest poyson couer,
That kiles more quicke then s[oo]words,
A faithfull harted louer[,]/
But you great godes [god] aboue
Knoues whot great plages beloneth,
to wronge trouelouers in there loue,
licke this fales harted woman,

But goe thy waye fonde frind,
Of this thy conquest bost thee
Thy false[w]hood makes me glad,
That I so soone haue lost thee,
I thinke that tiborne tree
with halter neuer hangeman,
That was more false of hart then thee,
Thou foule false harted woman,

Hast thou bine true to mee,

9 *mee*] interlined above deletion with caret   *[m]*] interlined above *a* in *any*
Fol. 60b   25 *Should*] *l* altered from long *s*   *foulest*] *s* altered, ? from *e*   30–1 squeezed in, ? added   30 *trouelouers*] [1]*e* added   34 *false[w]hood*] [2]*o* interlined with caret   37 *hangeman*] *g* altered from *d*

As I to thee am constant,
I neuer would haue left thee,
In ioy nor sorrowes instant,
But neuer I will beleue thee
That thou for loue art dying,
Therefore the les I greue,
At thy forse forged lying,

The lofty ciprus tre, [FOL. 61a]
That grouse so houge and statly
In licknes is to thee to thee,
Thou hast betrayed mee slatly,
For licke the tree that groeth,
And full of frut are barren,
A traytor hast thou bine,
A foule decemling carrion,

Seeke out thy mates else where,
And with desemling woe them,
And as thou hast done mee
Soe doe them and vndoe them
And then theyer songe will be,
The same that I haue songe,
That curse ildes the licke of thee,
Thou foule false harted tonge,

This my forsaken songe,
I draue vnto conclucion,
Though thou has dune mee wronge,
I wish not thy confucion,
But this I wish to thee,
Of bodi being slender,
That thy next loue may quit my greife,
and may my loue remember,

Writen by a gentelman that cares
as littel for the popes curse as the diuels blesing
Made by Iohn band in prison at heriford against
his loue sibbel hopper

43 *In*] *n* formed as incomplete *m* 44 *But*] *B* altered from *b* *I*] altered from *i* 45, 47 *dying . . . lying*] *y* dotted 51 *slatly*] ? for *flatly* 54 *traytor*] *y* dotted, ? altered from *i* 55 *decemling*] *c* altered from long *s* 60 *theyer*] *e* altered from *a*; *y* dotted, ? altered from *i* *will*] preceded by false start, long *s* 61 *songe*] *g* altered from *o* 66 *wronge*] interlined 68 *thee*] ^{2}*e* altered 70 *thy*] *h* altered *greife*] ^{1}*e* added 73 ^{2}*as*] *s* altered *blesing*] interlined

Memorandū that Margeret verch howell wido⟨w⟩ [Fol. 61b]
returned tenaunt vnto me the viijth day
of September 1619 in the p̄ͬsens of
Ienkin lloyd Esquier, Evan Glinne gent
Giles Iarman, David Powell & Hary
Evans my brother./

[Blank] [Fol. 62a]

Oer ddig pob musig, pob messvr siyn gas [Fol. 62b]
ar danne na ffibe ni chlowa i fawr flas
ni wn i mor rhagor rhwng llais Cvttarn dlos
ne delni, na thestni dyllvan liw nos

Ymmeth lywenvdd dos kerdd o ddiwrth i
tyrd briddder ath fwvnder maen gresso wrth i ti,
dy feirio am gellweirio y rowan i rwi
ni spendia i mor ofer mom amser yn hwv

Ni welir ond odid ienctvd yn brvdd
llawen fvdd gwvr ifenc liw nos a lliw didd
er y mod yn ifanc nid llawen wv fi
cymwvs iwr pryssvr fessvr [fessvr] ym fi

---

ffrvnd beth fellv'r ffrvnd anwvl, fel keffvl ich keir
a gnv'r ffrwvn ai ddannedd beth byn̄a ar a wneir
chwv lankes nech meistres im sarrig y svdd
ni wn ddim ond hynnv ach pare mor brvdd

---

ni dwdwi mor ynfvd heb ddyuedvd mvwn bost
nag wvlo ne grio ne dvchan mor dost
er mwvn llankes birrwen er dicked i thro
nid llygad svr llankes, am gvr i om ko

---

nid fi ydiwr dvn er melvn i thop
na'll fwvtta mor ffigis melvs or shop
na chysgv mvwn gwelv [(och ffoled i ben)] er mwvn llankes wen
ond tvchan a gwilied i lyged oi' ben

Fols. 62b, 63a Hand unidentified, ? resembles A
5 *lywenvdd*] *v* altered from *o* 8 *ofer*] *f* written over false start *mom*] ²*m* altered from *n* 9 *Ni*] *N* altered from *n* *brvdd*] *v* altered, ? from *o* 14 *byn̄a*] *y* altered 17 *ni dwdwi*] *sic* *ddyuedvd*] *yu* altered from *w*; *v* altered from *i* 19 *birrwen*] *w* altered 23 *er . . . wen*] interlined above deletion

---

ffrvnd. gwn rowan yr achos y soweth y svdd
eisie gweled my syfed ach gnaeth wchi mor brvdd
cewch i gweled Cam hvnnv mae arnoch beth bai
kin dowad ai blesser ai fwvnder mis mai

---

rwv j yn drwm am adel mam anwvl a thad [Fol. 63a]
a thrwm cawn am adel fy holl ffriends am gwlad
ni diw hvn ddim colled, i golled yn car
pen golles i gwmpni daeth atta i rvw far

---

tristwch ir amser i gydawodd e'r tir
can tristwch ir seren a svrodd fy sir
tristwch ir llongwvr, ai hwvle ai hor
ai helpodd i passio i rwvfo tros for

Can tristwch ir gwvnt ai awel laes wan [laes]
na thorse foe' whvle kin i fyned fo ir lan
nwsk kernod gwvddelod, nassiwn wvllt ffol
na ddel ai danfonodd bvth yn ihol

---

on i ddel e ym vsk i holl ffrvnds i gid
on i ddel e i gvmrv phenix y bvd
ni welir ar ene, wen er mwvn kar
na llywenvdd kalon ffrvnd ffyddlon ai par

Os oes neb a ofvn fel llygoden mwvn kist
er mwvn kar anwvl pwv a gane mor drist
dyn prydd a glaskodd i synwvr yng hvd
a dvn na fvdd lawen on i ddel tro⟨[.]⟩ar fvd

A briefe of my bookes & such things I left [Fol. 63b]
behinde mee in my study at my goinge home,
wich I Committed to the Custidy of Sir Walwine
Lau: Elegant:
Cleanarde

25 *svdd*] *v* altered, ? from *o*

Fol. 63a 8 *tros*] *r* altered from first loop of false start for *h* 9 *laes*] interlined with caret 13 *ffrvnds*] *v* altered from *u* 16 *ffrvnd*] *v* altered from *u* 17 *mwvn*] *wv* altered from *uw* *kist*] added in paler ink

Fol. 63b Hand A: list in single column, with pen tests and scribbles to right and two words of mirror writing at foot 1 *left*] *ft* altered from *ave*

Chil: Dictionary
Tuscil: quæst:
Nowel: Chat:
Mantuan:
Dia: Sacr:
Terentius
Tull: Rhet:
Deus et Rex
Tull: Ora:
Novus Test: La:
Ovidij Meta:
Text: Epith;
Aptho: p*ro*gim:
Linsy wolsy

---

a black Cloth
briches

---

2 inke botles
A standish

[Blank] [Fol. 64a]

[Blank] [Fol. 64b]

10 *Sacr :*] *c* altered from *r*, with extra stroke above 12 *Rhet :*] *h* added 21 *briches*] *e* altered, ? from *t*
Fol. 64b Sequences of numbers written at right-angles above blottings and pen shapes